# Vietnamese

*For my mother and father, who, aboard the* Empress of England,
*encouraged the beginnings of my culinary journeys, long before I could speak.*

# Vietnamese

fragrant and exotic: a deliciously simple cuisine

Ghillie Başan

with photography by
Martin Brigdale

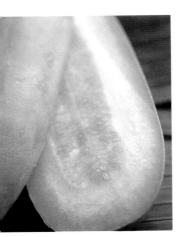

This edition is published by Aquamarine

Aquamarine is an imprint of Anness Publishing Ltd
Hermes House, 88–89 Blackfriars Road, London SE1 8HA
tel. 020 7401 2077; fax 020 7633 9499
www.aquamarinebooks.com; info@anness.com
© Anness Publishing Ltd 2004

UK agent: The Manning Partnership Ltd, 6 The Old Dairy,
Melcombe Road, Bath BA2 3LR; tel. 01225 478444;
fax 01225 478440; sales@manning-partnership.co.uk

UK distributor: Grantham Book Services Ltd, Isaac Newton
Way, Alma Park Industrial Estate, Grantham, Lincs NG31
9SD; tel. 01476 541080; fax 01476 541061;
orders@gbs.tbs-ltd.co.uk

North American agent/distributor: National Book Network,
4501 Forbes Boulevard, Suite 200, Lanham, MD 20706;
tel. 301 459 3366; fax 301 429 5746; www.nbnbooks.com

Australian agent/distributor: Pan Macmillan Australia, Level
18, St Martins Tower, 31 Market St, Sydney, NSW 2000;
tel. 1300 135 113; fax 1300 135 103;
customer.service@macmillan.com.au

New Zealand agent/distributor: David Bateman Ltd,
30 Tarndale Grove, Off Bush Road, Albany, Auckland;
tel. (09) 415 7664; fax (09) 415 8892

Publisher: Joanna Lorenz

Editorial Director: Judith Simons

Senior Editor: Susannah Blake

Photographer: Martin Brigdale

Home Economist: Lucy McKelvie

Stylist: Helen Trent

Designer: Louise Clements

Editorial Reader: Rosanna Fairhead

Production Controller: Wendy Lawson


10 9 8 7 6 5 4 3 2 1

NOTES
Bracketed terms are intended for American readers.

For all recipes, quantities are given in both metric and imperial
measures and, where appropriate, measures are also given in
standard cups and spoons. Follow one set, but not a mixture,
because they are not interchangeable.

Standard spoon and cup measures are level.
1 tsp = 5ml, 1 tbsp = 15ml, 1 cup = 250ml/8fl oz

Australian standard tablespoons are 20ml. Australian readers
should use 3 tsp in place of 1 tbsp for measuring small
quantities of gelatine, flour, salt, etc.

Medium (US large) eggs are used unless otherwise stated.

# Contents

# The country, culture and cuisine

Writers, poets and journalists who have written about the countries of former Indo-China, namely Cambodia, Laos and Vietnam, often talk about the people, their culture and cuisine with warmth and loyalty. When capturing the atmosphere of French-occupied Saigon, the descriptions are filled with the intoxicating perfumes, the lazy heat cooled by bursts of heavy, tropical rain, the colours that sing in shades of turquoise, saffron and jade, and the flashes of black, silken hair and light, traditional costumes, floating behind bicycles or weaving through markets.

The reality, though, is that Vietnam and its people are stoic survivors. Touched with tragedy and having survived the impact of lengthy wars, followed by hardship under Communist rule and, finally, the inevitable modernization by the West, Vietnam has risen from the ruins with its spirit intact. Today, from the border with China in the north to the rice mills of the Mekong Delta in the south, this long, narrow land of swollen rivers and lush, green paddy fields hums with activity.

Since the opening of Vietnam to tourism, there has been a new wave of excitement in all aspects of the culture, with a growing interest in the cuisine. Also, with the spread of Vietnamese refugees to different corners of the world, authentic restaurants have sprung up in Sydney, Paris, California and Florida, all presenting an intriguing fusion of flavours and history.

Indo-China has been described as a bewitching medley of the senses, and the same could be said of Vietnamese food. If you ask a Vietnamese cook where his fascinating cuisine originated from, he might, quite justifiably, reply, "from our ancestors". Like every culture with strong culinary roots, the influences can be traced back through several centuries, and the flavours, techniques and traditions are many and varied. In Vietnam's case, the evolution of its food and cooking can be found in a cross-cultural mixing bowl of legends, myths, invaders, rulers and indigenous peoples – each one adding their own subtle nuances to create a truly intriguing and colourful cuisine.

*Below: There is something unmistakable about the hum and bustle of Vietnam's busy streets, such as in Hanoi, the capital city.*

*Right: Fish and shellfish are part of the Vietnamese staple diet, and fishing boats are a common sight on the coast and rivers.*

Over the centuries, ancient empires have risen and fallen, but it was probably the Chinese who made the first dramatic impact on the culinary history of Vietnam. They ruled Vietnam for a thousand years from before 100BC until AD939, and made a profound mark on the Vietnamese culture and cuisine.

When the Chinese first conquered the Red River Delta in the north, they encountered the Viet, a nomadic, clan-based society, similar to the hill tribes today, who were reliant on hunting and fishing. With little opposition from these nomadic people, the Chinese laid down firm, powerful roots for the culture and government of Nam Viet, as well as for the development of its cuisine. The early kingdoms of Champa, in the centre, and Funan, in the south, also helped to lay the foundations and influence the development of the cuisine.

Through commercial relations with India, the flourishing kingdoms adopted Hinduism, employed Sanskrit as a sacred language, were influenced by Indian art and began trading in spices. The Chinese taught the Vietnamese ancestor-worship, Confucianism and Buddhism with its inherent vegetarian beliefs. They also taught the art of chopsticks and stir-frying in oil, the use of noodles, ginger, soy sauce and tofu and, of utmost importance, the cultivation of rice.

In the 10th century, the Mongol tribesmen came to Vietnam. They brought with them their love of beef, which led to the creation of the wonderful Vietnamese beef noodle soup, *pho*. By this time, Cambodia had become Indianized too, resulting in the development of the spicy southern cuisine. From Thailand and Laos, the emerging Vietnam borrowed shrimp paste, lemon grass, basil and mint, and combined them with Indian spices.

In the 16th century, European explorers from Portugal and Spain brought foods from the New World, including tomatoes, peanuts, corn and chillies. These vegetables and legumes grew with ease in the tropical soil and were swiftly cultivated and incorporated into the developing cuisine.

While Vietnam continued to trade with neighbouring Thailand, Laos and Cambodia, the arrival of the French in the mid-19th century had a refining influence on the cuisine. The French ruled there for nearly a hundred years, and during this time passed on their traditional techniques of sautéing and simmering for stock-making, as well as introducing asparagus, avocados, artichokes, frogs' legs, pâté, butter, yogurt, wine, beer, ice cream, café au lait and baguettes.

## Regional influences

The geographic split of this slender country has a strong impact on the regional differences in the cuisine. As the Vietnamese will point out, the country is shaped like a *don ganh*, the traditional bamboo pole slung over the shoulder with a basket of rice hanging from each end. These baskets represent the rice bowls of Vietnam: the Red River Delta in the north and the vast Mekong Delta in the south, connected by a mountainous spine.

Stretching from tip to tip on the eastern side is 2,400km/1,500 miles of coastline, which, in addition to the numerous flowing rivers and streams that carve through the land, provides Vietnam with such a volume of water that it has a steady supply of its two most important ingredients: rice and the fermented fish sauce, *nuoc mam*. With these two treasures the Vietnamese can go anywhere and cook themselves a satisfying meal; without them they are lost.

In the harsh, mountainous region of northern Vietnam, the cuisine is closely aligned with that of China. There is still a large Chinese population residing in this region, where the emphasis is on contrasting flavours and textures within the meal, a legacy from the Chinese occupation. The food is less complex than that of the central region and milder than the spicy dishes of the south.

*Above: In the markets of Saigon, stalls are laden with freshly baked baguettes, which are eaten almost as much as rice and noodles.*

Instead, northern cookery relies heavily on mild, aromatic black pepper and the indigenous herbs, which include basil, mint and coriander (cilantro). The best rice rolls, *banh cuon*, are reputed to come from Hanoi, the principal city of the north. Snail dishes are also popular in Hanoi, where the pond-dwelling creature grows to the size of a ping-pong ball, nicely fat for the local favourite, *bun oc*, boiled snails with noodles and *nuoc mam*. Other snail dishes include snails stewed in beer, *oc hap bia*, and minced snails to make savoury balls, *oc ngoi*, which are rolled in ginger leaves and then steamed in their shells. The communal dish, *lau*, which is often translated as hotpot but is in fact more akin to the French meat fondue, is attributed to the north and adopted from the Chinese, as is the national favourite noodle soup, *pho*, and the classic fish dish, *cha ca*. Sticky rice and sweet snacks made with mung beans are also specialities of Hanoi.

In central Vietnam, a variety of crops are grown, such as aubergines (eggplant), bitter melons, pumpkins, asparagus,

mangoes, pineapples, strawberries and artichokes. Game birds, river fish and shellfish are also in abundant supply. The food and cooking of the region makes excellent use of the local ingredients and ranges from simple dishes that can be enjoyed as everyday fare, to the more sophisticated dishes that originated in the kitchens of Hue.

Of all the cities in Vietnam, there is none so representative of culture and learning as the historic garden city of Hue, with its shady palm-fringed villas and the River of Perfumes cutting through the middle. Once the imperial city, controlling central Vietnam in the 19th century, Hue also dominated the food culture and was considered the centre of haute cuisine. The emperor Tu Doc, who reigned from 1848 to 1883, demanded extraordinary levels of energy and ingenuity from his kitchens, resulting in a highly refined cuisine. He expected 50 dishes to be prepared by 50 cooks and served by 50 servants at each meal, and he was not to be presented with the same meal twice in a year.

In Hue today, service remains formal and food is still presented in many small bowls as if feeding the emperor. Here you might find crab claws stuffed with pork, beef wrapped in wild betel leaves, and *chao tom* – minced prawn (shrimp) wrapped around sugar cane. These are dishes that appear elsewhere in Vietnam, but in Hue their presentation is of the utmost importance.

The food of the southern region is most typically found in the city of Saigon (now officially named Ho Chi Minh City, but fondly called by its old name), which in the 14th century was an Indianized Khmer town called Prey Nokor. Saigon was taken by the Vietnamese in the 18th century, by the French in the 19th century and once again by the Vietnamese in the 20th century. In this centre of commerce and trade, the cuisine shows the clear and distinct influences of the Chinese, Indians and colonial French. The food is vibrant and robust and the markets busy, relying heavily on the rice bowl and pastures of the Mekong Delta for produce.

The majority of the foodstuffs in the south comes from the countryside around Dalat, an area of cool mountain air, pine forests and warm sun. Just about anything grows here, including avocados, white strawberries, peaches, cauliflowers, tomatoes, tropical fruits and green salad vegetables, all of which are incorporated in the region's enticing dishes, which are served with French bread almost as often as with rice or noodles. Coconuts and sugar cane provide the base for many dishes, and tangy fruits are often added to salads and stir-fries. Clay pots, which were originally used by farmers and fishermen to cook a simple, tasty meal over a fire, are also particular to the area.

With such diverse inspiration – from the skilful culinary techniques of the Chinese and the light, sophisticated accents of the French, to the aromatic spices of India and Thailand – the resulting dishes are wholly unique. A stroll through a Saigon market shows all these influences together in perfect harmony. First, there is the addictive aroma of *pho*, the Chinese-inspired noodle soup, emanating from a small wooden stall. Next to it is a cart laden with warm, freshly baked baguette halves smeared with an aromatic, French-inspired pork pâté, and further on is the mouthwatering lure of sweet, plump prawns stir-fried in fragrant lemon grass and pungent Indian spices. The contrasting flavours and textures of sweet basil leaves, roasted peanuts, garlic and ginger, perfumed mint, banana blossom, lotus seeds and shredded green papaya contribute to a rich tapestry of exotic aromas and delicious dishes.

Taking pleasure in all aspects of food production, from the growing to the buying, preparing, cooking and eating, is an integral part of Vietnamese culture, highlighted in the proverb *hoc an, hoc noi*, which suggests that people should learn to eat before learning to speak.

## The bold palate

As well as the classic dishes such as *pho* and *cha gio* (spring rolls), which are eaten all day, every day, there are many unusual offerings that may be less appealing to the western palate. There is very little that the Vietnamese don't eat, and every part of the animal is used, even those bits other cultures discard. The flesh of dogs, the bladders of fish, the testicles of cocks, crunchy insects, wriggling geckos or the heart of a venomous snake are all part of the daily fare. If you desire monkey, you can have it slain and grilled before your eyes. Bats, toads, mice and rats; sparrows and turtledoves; crocodiles; bears and porcupines; and pythons and cobras are all on the menu. There are even restaurants where you can eye up your prey. Some of the rare delicacies are expensive and eating them is an opportunity to display wealth.

Within the Vietnamese culture, there are strong beliefs that certain foods have medicinal and aphrodisiac properties. The still-beating heart of a snake, washed down with its blood, is said to

*Below: In the daily markets, you will find every kind of food – from fresh fruit and vegetables to more exotic and unusual fare.*

increase sexual potency; a glass of viperine – rice wine with a whole venomous snake soused in it – is considered to jump-start a lazy libido; and dog eaten at the end of each lunar month is believed to warm the blood and bring good fortune, as well as ease the suffering of menstruating women.

The live markets, which may not appeal to the more squeamish, provide a degree of entertainment as well as a culinary education. On one side of the street you will see a coconut stall, where the young, green fruit are expertly whacked in half to give you a sip of fresh juice and a mouthful of the soft flesh, while on the other are cages of quacking ducks, clucking hens and honking geese, all tied together by their feet. You will see fish and prawns swimming in tanks, and hear knives being sharpened and cleavers thudding as fresh produce is prepared for the pot. This is part of Vietnamese life, and a fascinating experience.

*Below: Sticky rice cakes filled with pork and lotus seeds and steamed in lotus leaves are a popular celebration dish.*

## Festivals and celebrations

Vietnam's calendar is full of holidays and banquets, in addition to the usual family weddings and celebrations, all of which call for elaborate feasting and great celebration. A great deal of preparation goes into these events so that the food is overflowing. Each different festival calls for traditional specialities, and often the more time-consuming and fiddly dishes will also be prepared as a big treat. Opulent dishes will appear, such as the Vietnamese roast duck, sliced into juicy slabs, drizzled with the piquant fish sauce *nuoc cham* and wrapped in lettuce leaves; sticky rice cakes steamed in lotus leaves and decorated with lotus flowers; and highly prized fish, grilled or steamed whole, with the head presented to the guest who is destined for good fortune. On these occasions, the habitual fragrant tea may be cast aside for a little merriment with beer and wine.

*Below: Egg-shaped dumplings filled with sugar, known as* banh tro*, are served on the third lunar day of the third lunar month.*

The main holiday is *Tet*, the Vietnamese lunar New Year, a time of renewing and reaffirming beliefs in life, love, family and community. It is considered a physical and spiritual rebirth, a purification of the soul, involving many cleansing rituals. The full name is *Nguyen Dan*, which means new dawn, and it is celebrated with a three-day holiday commencing on the night of the first new moon of the calendar year. Seven days before this New Year, the *Tet* rites begin with the ascension of the Spirits of the Hearth (the kitchen gods) to the heavens, where they report on the past year's events to the Jade Emperor. On their journey these spirits are said to ride on the backs of fish, so people all over Vietnam release live carp into the rivers and lakes and lay offerings of food, fresh water, flowers and burning incense at the altars, all in the hope that the spirits will report kindly and bring back good fortune for the coming year.

The first meal of *Tet* is one for the ancestors because they are believed to have returned to the world of the living. The head of the family offers a grace, lights three incense sticks, then invites five generations of the deceased to join in the family feast by whispering their names. This ceremony of ancestor calling takes place at the morning and evening meals for the three days of *Tet*.

The second day of *Tet* involves visiting the wife's family and close friends, and the third day is for embracing the community. Families visit the schoolteachers, patients visit their doctors, and many people visit astrologers to hear the fortunes of the new year.

On the evening of the third day, the ancestors depart. The principal *Tet* speciality is *banh chung*, sticky rice cakes filled with bean paste and, traditionally, wrapped in a parcel made from a green *dong* (similar to a banana leaf) and tied with bamboo twine. Throughout the festivities, stacks of *banh chung* are piled high in the shops and market stalls, where other *Tet* favourites, such as watermelons and dragon fruit, assortments of sweets, lotus seeds that have been dyed a festive red to represent joy, truth and sincerity, and the popular *mut*, a candied concoction of vegetables and dried fruits, are all on display among woven, painted masks. Lucky money is placed on trees as offerings to the ancestors, and homes are decorated with trees, such as pretty, fruit-laden kumquats or peach and apricot trees resplendent in perfumed blossom, to ward off evil spirits.

As well as the New Year festivities, there are many other smaller festivals, often occuring on the full moon. *Hai Ba Trung* occurs on the sixth day of the second lunar month and celebrates the revolt of the Trung sisters against the Chinese in AD40. *Thanh minh* is the holiday of the dead. Vietnamese pay homage to their deceased ancestors and relatives on this day, and visit their graves making

*Above: Three incense sticks are always lit to mark the first meal on the first day of the New Year* Tet *celebrations.*

offerings of food, flowers and incense. *Doan ngu*, summer solstice, falls on the fifth day of the fifth moon and offerings are made to the spirit world to ward off pestilence and disease. The mid-autumn festival, *tet trung thu*, is a children's festival and marks a day of much celebrating. Vietnamese folklore has it that parents have worked so hard bringing in the harvest that this is a day specifically for children.

On *trung nguyen*, day of the wandering souls, the spirits of the dead are believed to inhabit the residence of their offspring so offerings are made to the household altars for the souls of the deceased and paper money is burnt in their honour.

On the third day of the third lunar month there is a festival at which the Vietnamese eat only cold food. The celebration is based on a legend about a loyal servant who cut off a part of his own thigh and grilled it for his starving prince. Later, when the prince

*Above: In Vietnam, it is always polite for a guest to bring a small gift, such as a bunch of flowers, for their host.*

became king, he forgot all about the loyal servant and his selfless deed. Disheartened, the servant sought refuge in the jungle. One day, the king did remember him and tried to coax him out, but the servant refused to budge. The king had the jungle set on fire to force him out; however, the servant stayed put and was burnt to death instead. To honour the servant and his unjust fate, the Vietnamese eat cold foods, such as sticky-rice dumplings and raw salads, for three days – the duration of a traditional wake.

One of the specialities for this holiday is *banh tro*, a slightly sweet egg-shaped rice dumpling with a little pellet of brown sugar in the middle. The rice shell surrounding the sugar represents the heavens and the sweet centre represents the earth. The shape of the dumplings is also significant to Vietnamese beliefs. In legend, the Vietnamese people are said to have been descended from the union of a mountain spirit and a water dragon, which resulted in a hundred eggs that hatched into a hundred sons.

## Traditional dining

Because eating plays such an important role in Vietnamese society, there are certain dining traditions, although these can vary from region to region. For example, in northern and central Vietnam, it is customary for the oldest family member to sit nearest the door and everyone else to be arranged in descending age order. The eldest will also be the first to help him or herself to food, and a host will often serve the guest. In the south, where dining etiquette is more relaxed, everyone is encouraged to serve themselves.

If you are the guest, it is important to bring a small gift. Whether you are invited to eat in a restaurant or a home, it is polite throughout Asia to bring your host a little box of something sweet or a bunch of fresh flowers. However, in Vietnam it is important not to bring white flowers because this signifies death.

As with most Asian countries, dining is a communal affair. A selection of dishes may be put on a table and each diner will be given their own individual bowl into which the food is spooned. When passing the food around, two hands are used to hold the dish and the exchange is acknowledged with a nod. Food is usually eaten with the fingers, chopsticks or spoons, although the Vietnamese have a knack of sipping their food from the spoon without ever putting the spoon into their mouths. The proper way to eat is to take some rice from the communal dish and put it into your bowl, then use the ceramic spoon to transfer the meat, fish or vegetables on to your rice. Hold the bowl up near to your mouth and use the chopsticks to scoop in the tasty morsels. It is polite for the host to offer more food than the guests can eat but, equally, it is polite for the guests not to eat everything in sight and to leave a little food in the bowl to show that they have eaten enough.

A typical family meal in Vietnam will consist of a large bowl of rice and three or four other dishes – perhaps a bowl of the cleansing broth, *cahn*, a meat or fish dish, and a vegetable dish or salad – to provide a balance of starch, protein and vegetables, as well as colour, taste and texture. Depending on the complexity of the meal, there will be a number of individual dipping bowls containing sweet or spicy condiments, and there may also be bowls of chillies or pickled vegetables to crunch and chew on between mouthfuls. All the dishes are served together. Fresh fruit, rather than a dessert, is usually offered at the end of the meal.

When the Vietnamese eat, there is a great deal of gutsy enjoyment and noisy slurping. Eating is almost a game – there are crabs to crack, prawns to suck, food to be wrapped and rolled, and a great deal of mess and merriment – the Vietnamese love to linger over food.

## Tea and coffee

These two drinks are an important part of the Vietnamese culture and way of life. Tea plays a significant role in business as well as in general social life. An offer of tea, in a home or place of work, in the bank or in the market, is a gesture of hospitality that it is polite to accept. Everybody drinks tea, and the sharing of it is almost ritualistic. It is usually drunk black and, in some homes, its preparation can turn into quite a performance.

The Thai Binh Province has its own celebration of tea, where enthusiasts set off in boats in the moonlight when the lotus flowers are in bloom. Each flower is prised open and a pinch of tea placed inside. By dawn the fragrance of the lotus blossom will have permeated the tea, which is gathered to add to the teapots.

It was at Hue, during the Nguyen dynasty, that tea acquired art status. Whether it was drunk in the garden or in an intimate room, it would be served at a small table pushed against the wall so that there was room for only three people. To make tea in the traditional Hue way, a kettle is set over a charcoal brazier with aromatic wood for burning. Once boiling, it is removed to allow the water to cool to about 90°C/194°F, then poured over loose tea in a teapot. Once brewed, the tea is poured into the larger cup, called the commander cup, which is then used as the pouring vessel into the smaller ones, the soldier cups.

Coffee, by contrast, is a legacy of the French, but no less loved. In cities such as Saigon, you will find cafés filled with people sipping this unique brew. *Ca phe,* or *café vietnamien*, is a twist on the classic café au lait. When you sit down in a café, a glass tumbler with a little aluminium pot placed on top will be put before you. Sitting at the bottom of the tumbler is 1cm/½in of sweetened condensed milk, on to which splash little drips of coffee from the aluminium pot above. When the dripping stops, there will be a 1cm/½in layer of strong coffee on top of the condensed milk.

*Below: Vietnamese coffee made with condensed milk is a unique and utterly delicious drink that should be lingered over in a café.*

*Below: The traditional Hue method of making tea is a complex affair, involving one large pouring cup and three smaller ones.*

# Authentic cooking and essential flavours

The traditional Vietnamese kitchen is very basic. Often dark and sparsely kitted out, with an open hearth and few utensils, the focal point is the shrine for the kitchen god or other spiritual deities linked to this important room. Food is generally bought daily from the markets, taken home and cooked immediately so, unless you visit the kitchen during the frenzied moments of culinary activity over the hearth, there is little evidence of food or cooking.

Without refrigerators, fresh produce from the daily markets is vital. For many Vietnamese, two visits to the market are required: in the morning for the ingredients to cook for lunch and in the afternoon, for the evening meal. Back in the simple kitchen, the activity begins with the scrubbing of vegetables, the plucking and jointing of birds (if this hasn't already been done at the market), the endless chopping and slicing, and the pounding of herbs and spices in a mortar and pestle.

Woks and bamboo steamers are the primary pieces of equipment in the Vietnamese kitchen, but a solid mortar and pestle, a good set of cleavers, a hard surface for chopping, clay pots, wire baskets for noodles, bamboo chopsticks, muslin (cheesecloth) to make sticky rice, a charcoal grill, and a reliable water supply for the continual washing of ingredients and utensils are all essential. The large mortar and pestle, made of stone, is used not only for grinding spices, chillies and garlic, but also for pounding together all the condiments and pastes, as well as the meat for pâtés and savoury balls. Cleavers are important too; there are special blades for the fine chopping of lemon grass and green papaya, heavy blades for opening coconuts, thin ones for shredding spring onions (scallions), and multipurpose ones for any type of chopping, slicing and crushing. With these items, as well as a bit of time and patience, any Vietnamese dish can be prepared. The traditional cooking methods are simple too, with grilling over charcoal, simmering, steaming and deep-frying being the principal techniques.

*Below: The use of fragrant and intensely flavoured herbs, aromatics and spices helps to define and describe every Vietnamese dish.*

*Below: Banana blossom, frilly dried cloud ear (wood ear) mushrooms, and tart tamarind are all widely used ingredients.*

## Flavours and ingredients

While rice and *nuoc mam* form the foundations of the cuisine, herbs, spices and condiments are the building blocks. They have been part of the region's culinary history since AD166, when the Romans first landed there on the spice route. The Portuguese introduced New World spices, vegetables and fruit in the 16th and 17th centuries, and by the time the French arrived in the 19th century, these new ingredients had been cultivated for some time – so much so that younger generations had no idea that they were not indigenous to Vietnam.

The Vietnamese love to mix herbs, piling them on top of cooked dishes, wrapping them around tasty morsels and tucking them into rice wrappers. Among the herbs and spices are numerous varieties of mint, dill, coriander (cilantro), basil, thyme, oregano, chives, lemon grass, ginger, the liquorice-flavoured star anise, turmeric, fresh and dried chillies, galangal, garlic, and the Chinese five-spice powder, which is a blend of star anise, fennel, clove, cinnamon and pepper. Condiments such as raw vegetables pickled in rice vinegar and salt, flavoured oils, and potent pastes and sauces are equally important. These range from chilli paste and chilli sauce to pickled shallots, Chinese oyster sauce, anchovy sauce, curry paste, spring onion or garlic oil, soy sauce, shrimp paste, pickled pumpkin or radish, salted chillies and the Chinese hoisin sauce.

Other ingredients that shape Vietnamese cuisine include lotus roots and seeds, bananas, sugar cane, tofu, bean-sprouts, bitter melon, taro, bamboo shoots, dried cloud ear (wood ear) mushrooms, tiger lilies, water spinach, rice noodles and bean thread (cellophane) noodles, shallots, limes, coconuts and dried fish. Roasted, crushed peanuts are scattered over dishes. Spring onions, which appear in many dishes, are often cut into strips and added raw to soups, spring rolls and stir-fries. Chillies are used liberally – stir-fried, sliced finely and added to the herbs piled on top of soups and noodles, or eaten raw as a condiment. They are also used in many of the dipping sauces, including the ubiquitous *nuoc cham*. The chillies used most frequently in Vietnam are the small fiery red and green Thai varieties, and the longer, fatter, slightly less hot Serrano chillies. Because of the way the Vietnamese cook, the chillies are rarely in the pan for very long, preventing them from distributing too much of the powerful heat of which they are capable. However, having said that, some southern cooks take such a free hand with chillies that the dishes are extremely fiery.

The ingredient that is quintessentially Vietnamese is *nuoc mam*, a fermented fish sauce with a distinctive, pungent smell. It is splashed into practically every soup, stir-fry and marinade, as well

*Above: The pungent fish sauce,* nuoc mam, *and fiery red and green chillies are used in virtually every savoury Vietnamese dish.*

as being served as a standard dipping sauce. *Nuoc mam* is made from small fish layered with salt and fermented in barrels for about three months. The liquid that gathers in the base is then drained off and poured back over the fish to ferment for another three months. The liquid, which by this time is extremely pungent, is finally drained and strained into bottles, where it is left to mature even further. The odour is so strong that, along with the obnoxious-smelling fruit, durian, *nuoc mam* has been banned on Vietnam Airlines.

Despite its powerful smell, *nuoc mam* really does enhance the dish it's added to, lifting the flavours of other ingredients. It is available in most Asian and Chinese stores. Look for a rich, dark colour with the words *ngon* or *thuong hang* on the label, which indicate a superior quality. If you cannot find *nuoc mam*, Thai fish sauce, *nam pla*, is a useful alternative (although not quite the same). As well as *nuoc mam*, there are several condiments and dipping sauces – often flavoured with *nuoc mam* – such as *nuoc cham*, *nuoc leo*, *nuoc xa ot* and *nuoc mam gung*. These form an integral part of every Vietnamese meal so are well worth making.

## nuoc cham

There are many versions of this popular chilli dipping sauce, varying in degrees of sweet, sour and chilli. Some people add rice vinegar to the mix. Depending on the amount of liquid added, this recipe makes about 200ml/7fl oz/scant 1 cup, which is plenty for all the dishes in this book. If you don't use it all in one sitting, it will keep well in the refrigerator for about two weeks. If you are doing a lot of Vietnamese cooking, it is an extremely handy sauce to have ready-made in quantity.

4 garlic cloves, roughly chopped
2 red Thai chillies, seeded and
  roughly chopped
15–20ml/3–4 tsp sugar
juice of 1 lime
60ml/4 tbsp *nuoc mam*

1 Using a mortar and pestle, pound the garlic with the chillies and sugar and grind to make a paste.
2 Squeeze in the lime juice, add the *nuoc mam* and then stir in 60–75ml/4–5 tbsp water, according to taste. Blend well.

## nuoc leo

This hot peanut dipping sauce is popular throughout Vietnam. Add more chilli, sugar or liquid, according to taste. This recipe makes about 300ml/10fl oz/2¼ cups.

15ml/1 tbsp vegetable oil
1–2 garlic cloves, finely chopped
1–2 red Thai chillies, seeded and chopped
115g/4oz/⅔ cup unsalted roasted peanuts,
  finely chopped
150ml/¼ pint/⅔ cup chicken stock
60ml/4 tbsp coconut milk
15ml/1 tbsp hoisin sauce
15ml/1 tbsp *nuoc mam*
15ml/1 tbsp sugar

1 Heat the oil in a small wok and stir in the garlic and chillies. When they begin to colour, add all but 15ml/1 tbsp of the peanuts. Stir for a few minutes until the oil from the peanuts begins to weep.
2 Add the remaining ingredients, bring to the boil, then simmer until the sauce thickens and oil appears on the surface.
3 Transfer the sauce to a serving dish and garnish with the reserved peanuts.

## nuoc xa ot

This lemon grass, chilli and soy dipping sauce often accompanies fish dishes or fried tofu. It also makes a refreshing dipping sauce for roasted meats, as well as an alternative to the classic *nuoc cham* served with Vietnamese spring rolls. For most dishes you only need a small quantity. This recipe makes about 100ml/3½fl oz/ scant ½ cup.

30ml/2 tbsp vegetable oil
1 lemon grass stalk, leaves removed,
  finely chopped
1 garlic clove, crushed
2 spring onions (scallions), finely sliced
2 red Thai chillies, seeded
  and finely sliced
75–90ml/5–6 tbsp soy sauce

1 Heat the oil in a small wok or heavy pan and stir in the lemon grass, garlic, spring onions and chillies.
2 When the lemon grass begins to turn golden, quickly stir in the soy sauce. Remove the pan from the heat and pour the *nuoc xa ot* into a serving bowl.

## nuoc mam gung

This delicious, intensely flavoured ginger sauce is served as an accompaniment to grilled (broiled) or roasted poultry and fish dishes. It is also drizzled over plain noodles or rice to give them a little extra spike, and is a good sauce to serve with Vietnamese beef fondue. In this recipe, the ginger is grated, but it can be pounded to a pulp using a mortar and pestle, if you prefer. This recipe makes about 150ml/ ¼ pint/⅔ cup.

15ml/1 tbsp *nuoc mam*
juice of 1 lime
5ml/1 tsp honey
100ml/3½fl oz/scant ½ cup groundnut
  (peanut) or sesame oil
75g/3oz fresh root ginger, peeled
  and grated
2 red Thai chillies, seeded
  and finely chopped

1 In a bowl, mix the *nuoc mam* with the lime juice and honey, until well blended.
2 Beat in the oil, ginger and chillies, then leave to stand for at least 30 minutes.

## infused oils

Many classic Vietnamese dishes call for a flavoured oil to be brushed over noodles, grilled (broiled) meat or steamed pâtés, or to be drizzled over a dish such as soup before serving. Generally, this oil is infused with spring onions (scallions) or garlic. The garlic oil in particular has quite an intense flavour and aroma, so use it sparingly to taste. It is worth making up a batch of spring onion- or garlic-infused oil to have handy. This recipe makes 250ml/8fl oz/1 cup and can be stored in a sealed container in the refrigerator for 2–3 weeks.

250ml/8fl oz/1 cup vegetable
  or groundnut (peanut) oil
8 finely sliced spring onions (scallions)
  or 5 garlic cloves, crushed

1 Pour the oil into a pan and heat over a medium heat. Stir in the spring onions or garlic and remove the pan from the heat.
2 Leave to infuse until cool, then carefully pour the oil into a clean jar or bottle and seal tightly. Store in the refrigerator until ready to use.

## salted chillies with lime

This red-hot condiment, which is frequently found on Vietnamese tables, is not for the faint-hearted. In fact, it is only for those who like fire on their tongues and pain in their bellies. You will often find little dishes of chillies, salt and lime served as an accompaniment, which diners can dip into between mouthfuls of the main dish. They require little preparation and are a classic accompaniment, giving an authentic Vietnamese feel to any meal.

To prepare the salted chillies, simply cut a handful of green or red chillies in half lengthways and remove the seeds and white pith. Pile the seeded chillies on a plate, pour some sea salt on to the edge of the plate and place a lime, cut into equal segments, on the plate as well.

When you feel like bursting into flames, take a chilli and a wedge of lime and squeeze the juice over the chilli. Next dip the zesty chilli into the salt and pop it into your mouth. Many of your Vietnamese dining companions may be doing just that, with neither a tear in their eyes nor sweat on their brows.

Pho and other soups

# Broths and stocks

In Hanoi and Saigon (officially Ho Chi Minh City), the working day usually begins with the nation's favourite dish: *pho*, a rice noodle soup with beef. The spicy beef aroma wafting through the streets from noodle shops and soup stalls is so enticing that it is impossible not to be lured to a bowl of the clear, seasoned broth and velvety noodles. The origins of this classic noodle broth are believed to lie with the early Mongolian tribes in the north of Vietnam. However, it probably developed into such a fine dish in Hanoi only during the latter part of the 1800s.

The root of the word *pho* is said to be the French *feu*, from *pot-au-feu*, translated as "pot-on-the-fire". However, *pho* owes its creation both to the French – for the use of beef and the method of simmering bones to make a sophisticated broth – and to the Chinese, for their inclusion of ginger and noodles. When northern Vietnam fell under Communist control in 1954, almost a million people fled to the south, taking with them the secrets of *pho*. It didn't take long for the southerners to put their own stamp on the dish with a flourish of spices, chilli, lime, basil and beansprouts, giving it the Indo-Vietnamese character that is so entwined in the cuisine of the region.

Although *pho* could be considered the national dish of Vietnam, it is by no means the only soup. The Vietnamese love their soups and create both complex and simple ones, all of which fall into four main categories. *Canh* is a light, clear broth, infused with herbs, designed to refresh and cleanse the palate – it is served in a communal bowl and slurped from individual ceramic spoons in between bites of the main dish. *Sup* is a heartier, thickened broth, akin to a French *velouté*, and served as the appetizer to a meal. *Chao* is a nourishing, porridge-like soup of Chinese origin. Made with rice and served with spicy condiments and crunchy garnishes, *chao* is enjoyed as a belly-filler at any time of day. The final category is the classic noodle soup, *pho*, which, although principally made with beef, can be made with chicken, pork or seafood. *Pho* and *chao* are popular breakfast dishes as well as being enjoyed at all hours of the day and night, and there are numerous stalls everywhere you go in Vietnam where these hearty, fragrant meals are ladled out into colourful bowls.

Whichever soup is prepared, though, the emphasis is on the stock. If the stock is not meaty and tasty, the soup will be considered unsuccessful. Stock (bouillon) cubes, cooked scraps and short cuts will not achieve the right flavour; only the simmering

of fresh bones and meat, with perhaps a few vegetables and herbs and exotic spices, such as ginger, star anise, cloves and cinnamon, will attain the Vietnamese standards of subtlety and flavour.

Although the emphasis lies on the quality of the stock, the balance of flavours acquired from the ancient Chinese tradition of masking bitter with sweet, and strong with subtle, is of equal importance. This balancing of flavours is not only for the taste but also for diuretic and medicinal purposes. Generally, chicken or pork stocks, often infused with dried prawns (shrimp) or squid, are used as a base for most vegetable, poultry, fish and shellfish dishes. Fish and shellfish stocks, using the heads, tails, bones and shells, are used less frequently inland, but are a practical option in the fishing villages, where the traditional fish-head soup is common fare. Because of its relative expense, beef is reserved for stocks that will be used for a beef soup, and pure vegetable stocks really appear only in the diets of monks from certain Buddhist sects.

*Mi vit tim is a popular dish of aromatic broth with roast duck, pak choi and egg noodles (right). Green and red Thai chillies (opposite) and winter melon (top).*

# Beef noodle soup

Some would say that this classic noodle soup, *pho*, is Vietnam in a bowl. Made with beef (*pho bo*) or chicken (*pho ga*), it is Vietnamese fast food, street food, working men's food and family food. It is cheap and filling, and makes an intensely satisfying meal at any time of day or night. In the south, in particular, it is popular for breakfast. Everyone has their own recipe for *pho*, or their favourite place to enjoy it. But the key to *pho* is a tasty, light stock flavoured with ginger, cinnamon, cloves and star anise, so it is worth cooking it slowly and leaving it to stand overnight to allow the flavours to develop fully.

**serves 6**

250g/9oz beef sirloin

500g/1¼lb dried rice sticks
  (vermicelli), soaked in lukewarm
  water for 20 minutes

1 onion, halved and finely sliced

6–8 spring onions (scallions),
  cut into long pieces

2–3 red Thai chillies, seeded
  and finely sliced

115g/4oz/½ cup beansprouts

1 large bunch each of fresh
  coriander (cilantro) and mint,
  stalks removed, leaves chopped

2 limes, quartered, and hoisin sauce,
  *nuoc mam* or *nuoc cham* to serve

FOR THE STOCK

1.5kg/3lb 5oz oxtail, trimmed
  of fat and cut into thick pieces

1kg/2¼lb beef shank or brisket

2 large onions, peeled and quartered

2 carrots, peeled and cut into chunks

7.5cm/3in fresh root ginger,
  cut into chunks

6 cloves

2 cinnamon sticks

6 star anise

5ml/1 tsp black peppercorns

30ml/2 tbsp soy sauce

45–60ml/3–4 tbsp *nuoc mam*

salt

1 To make the stock, put the oxtail into a large, deep pan and cover it with water. Bring it to the boil and blanch the meat for 10–15 minutes. Drain the meat, rinsing off any scum, and clean out the pan. Put the blanched oxtail back into the pan with the other stock ingredients, apart from the *nuoc mam* and salt, and cover with about 3 litres/5¼ pints/12 cups water. Bring it to the boil, reduce the heat and simmer, covered, for 2–3 hours.

2 Remove the lid and simmer for another hour, until the stock has reduced to about 2 litres/3½ pints/8 cups. Skim off any fat and then strain the stock into another pan.

3 Cut the beef sirloin against the grain into very thin pieces, the size of the heel of a hand. Bring the stock to the boil once more, stir in the *nuoc mam*, season to taste with salt, then reduce the heat and leave the stock simmering gently until ready to use.

4 Meanwhile, bring a pan filled with water to the boil, drain the rice sticks and add to the water. Cook for about 5 minutes or until tender – you may need to separate them with a pair of chopsticks if they look as though they are sticking together.

5 Drain the rice sticks and divide them equally among six wide soup bowls. Top each serving with the slices of beef, onions, spring onions and chillies. Ladle the hot stock over the top of these ingredients, top with the beansprouts and fresh herbs and serve with the lime wedges to squeeze over. Pass around the hoisin sauce, *nuoc mam* or *nuoc cham* for those who like a little sweetening, fish flavouring or extra fire.

### serving pho

Every bowl of *pho* is lined with hot noodles and fine slices of rare, tender beef, which cooks gently under the steaming stock that is spooned over the top. To this you may add your own additional flavourings from the choice of garnishes. You may like crisp beansprouts, a sharp bite of spring onion, or a splash of garlic or chilli sauce. Then, using your chopsticks, lift the noodles through the layers of flavouring and slurp them up. This is the essence of Vietnam.

Nutritional information per portion: Energy 391Kcal/1635kJ; Protein 16g; Carbohydrate 74g, of which sugars 3g; Fat 2g, of which saturates 1g; Cholesterol 21mg; Calcium 62mg; Fibre 0.8g; Sodium 0.6g

# Saigon pork and prawn soup with rice sticks

Like *pho*, this soup, called *hu tieu do bien*, relies heavily on a richly flavoured stock. Without it the taste would be bland and insipid. *Hu tieu do bien* is a speciality of Saigon and the surrounding area, where the pork stock is enhanced with the intense sweet and smoky flavour of dried squid. To serve the soup as a meal on its own, add bite-size pieces of soaked dried shiitake mushrooms or cubes of firm tofu.

**serves 4**

225g/8oz pork tenderloin

225g/8oz dried rice sticks
(vermicelli), soaked in lukewarm
water for 20 minutes

20 prawns (shrimp), shelled
and deveined

115g/4oz/½ cup beansprouts

2 spring onions (scallions),
finely sliced

2 green or red Thai chillies, seeded
and finely sliced

1 garlic clove, finely sliced

1 bunch each of coriander (cilantro)
and basil, stalks removed, leaves
roughly chopped

1 lime, cut into quarters, and
*nuoc cham*, to serve

FOR THE STOCK

25g/1oz dried squid

675g/1½lb pork ribs

1 onion, peeled and quartered

225g/8oz carrots, peeled and cut
into chunks

15ml/1 tbsp *nuoc mam*

15ml/1 tbsp soy sauce

6 black peppercorns

salt

1 To make the stock, soak the dried squid in water for 30 minutes, rinse and drain. Put the ribs in a large pan and cover with approximately 2.5 litres/4½ pints/10 cups water. Bring the water to the boil, skim off any fat, and add the dried squid with the remaining stock ingredients. Cover the pan and simmer for 1 hour, then skim off any foam or fat and continue to simmer, uncovered, for a further 1½ hours.

2 Strain the stock and check the seasoning, adding a little more if necessary. You should have roughly 2 litres/3½ pints/8 cups.

3 Pour the stock into a wok or deep pan and bring to the boil. Reduce the heat, add the pork tenderloin and simmer for about 25 minutes. Carefully lift the tenderloin out of the stock, place it on a board and cut it into thin slices. Meanwhile, keep the stock simmering gently over a low heat.

4 Bring a pan of water to the boil. Drain the rice sticks and add to the water. Cook for about 5 minutes, or until tender, separating them with chopsticks if they stick together. Drain the rice sticks and divide them among four warm bowls.

5 Drop the prawns into the simmering stock for 1 minute. Lift them out with a slotted spoon and layer them with the slices of pork on top of the rice sticks. Ladle the hot stock over them and sprinkle with beansprouts, spring onions, chillies, garlic and herbs. Serve each bowl of soup with a wedge of lime to squeeze over it and *nuoc cham* to splash on top.

### dried squid

Look for the smoky dried squid in Chinese and Asian markets. If you cannot find it, you can use dried shrimp instead, which is usually easier to find. The shrimp will need to be soaked and drained in the same way as the squid.

Nutritional information per portion: Energy 319Kcal/1339kJ; Protein 22g; Carbohydrate 50g, of which sugars 1g; Fat 3g, of which saturates 0g; Cholesterol 49mg; Calcium 91mg; Fibre 0.6g; Sodium 0.5g

# Winter melon soup with tiger lilies

This simple soup uses two traditional South-east Asian ingredients – winter melon to absorb the flavours and tiger lilies to lift the broth with a floral scent. Both are available in Asian markets, but when choosing tiger lilies, make sure they are light golden in colour – sometimes they are referred to as golden needles. If you can't find winter melon, you could make the soup using another winter squash.

**serves 4**
350g/12oz winter melon
25g/1oz tiger lilies, soaked in hot
  water for 20 minutes
salt and ground black pepper
1 small bunch each of coriander
  (cilantro) and mint, stalks
  removed, leaves chopped,
  to serve

FOR THE STOCK
25g/1oz dried shrimp, soaked
  in water for 15 minutes
500g/1¼lb pork ribs
1 onion, peeled and quartered
175g/6oz carrots, peeled and cut
  into chunks
15ml/1 tbsp *nuoc mam*
15ml/1 tbsp soy sauce
4 black peppercorns

1 To make the stock, drain and rinse the dried shrimp. Put the pork ribs in a large pan and cover with 2 litres/3½ pints/8 cups water. Bring the water to the boil, skim off any fat, and add the dried shrimp and the remaining stock ingredients. Cover and simmer for 1½ hours, then skim off any foam or fat. Continue simmering, uncovered, for a further 30 minutes. Strain and check the seasoning. You should have about 1.5 litres/2½ pints/6¼ cups.

2 Halve the winter melon lengthways and remove the seeds and inner membrane. Finely slice the flesh into half-moons. Squeeze the soaked tiger lilies dry and tie them in a knot.

3 Bring the stock to the boil in a deep pan or wok. Reduce the heat and add the winter melon and tiger lilies. Simmer for 15–20 minutes, or until the winter melon is tender. Season to taste, scatter the coriander and mint over the top, and serve immediately.

Nutritional information per portion: Energy 46Kcal/198kJ; Protein 2g; Carbohydrate 9g, of which sugars 4g; Fat 0g, of which saturates 0g; Cholesterol 0mg; Calcium 90mg; Fibre 1.4g; Sodium 0.4g

# Tofu soup with mushrooms, tomato, ginger and coriander

This is a typical *canh* – a clear broth from the north of Vietnam. It is designed to be light, to balance a meal that may include some heavier meat or poultry dishes. As the soup is reliant on a well-flavoured, aromatic broth, the basic stock needs to be rich in taste.

1 To make the stock, put the chicken carcass or pork ribs in a deep pan. Drain and rinse the dried squid or shrimp. Add to the pan with the remaining stock ingredients, except the salt, and pour in 2 litres/3½ pints/8 cups water. Bring the water to the boil, and boil for a few minutes, skim off any foam, then reduce the heat and simmer gently with the lid on for 1½–2 hours. Remove the lid and continue simmering for a further 30 minutes to reduce. Skim off any fat, season with salt, then strain and measure out 1.5 litres/2½ pints/6¼ cups.

2 Squeeze dry the soaked shiitake mushrooms, remove the stems and slice the caps into thin strips. Heat the oil in a large pan or wok and stir in the shallots, chilli and ginger. As the fragrance begins to rise, stir in the *nuoc mam*, followed by the stock.

3 Add the tofu, mushrooms and tomatoes and bring the stock to the boil. Reduce the heat and simmer for 5–10 minutes. Season to taste and scatter the finely chopped fresh coriander over the top. Serve piping hot.

**serves 4**

115g/4oz/scant 2 cups dried shiitake mushrooms, soaked in water for 20 minutes

15ml/1 tbsp vegetable oil

2 shallots, halved and sliced

2 Thai chillies, seeded and sliced

4cm/1½in fresh root ginger, peeled and grated or finely chopped

15ml/1 tbsp *nuoc mam*

350g/12oz tofu, rinsed, drained and cut into bitesize cubes

4 tomatoes, skinned, seeded and cut into thin strips

salt and ground black pepper

1 bunch of coriander (cilantro), stalks removed, finely chopped, to garnish

FOR THE STOCK

1 meaty chicken carcass or 500g/1¼lb pork ribs

25g/1oz dried squid or shrimp, soaked in water for 15 minutes

2 onions, peeled and quartered

2 garlic cloves, crushed

7.5cm/3in fresh root ginger, coarsely chopped

15ml/1 tbsp *nuoc mam*

6 black peppercorns

2 star anise

4 cloves

1 cinnamon stick

sea salt

Nutritional information per portion: Energy 220Kcal/919kJ; Protein 12g; Carbohydrate 26g, of which sugars 4g; Fat 8g, of which saturates 1g; Cholesterol 0mg; Calcium 47.8mg; Fibre 1.1g; Sodium 0.5g

# Light and fragrant broth with stuffed cabbage leaves

The origins of this soup, called *canh bap cuon*, could be attributed to the French dish *chou farci*, or to the ancient Chinese tradition of cooking dumplings in a clear broth. Whatever the source, this classic Vietnamese soup takes a little time to prepare, so it is often reserved for special occasions such as the New Year, *Tet*. Each cabbage leaf is blanched, then rolled into a bitesize bundle with a mushroom, minced pork and shrimp filling. It is then tied securely with blanched spring onions.

### serves 4

10 Chinese leaves (Chinese cabbage) or Savoy cabbage leaves, halved, main ribs removed

4 spring onions (scallions), green tops left whole, white part finely chopped

5–6 dried cloud ear (wood ear) mushrooms, soaked in hot water for 15 minutes

115g/4oz minced (ground) pork

115g/4oz prawns (shrimp), shelled, deveined and finely chopped

1 Thai chilli, seeded and chopped

30ml/2 tbsp *nuoc mam*

15ml/1 tbsp soy sauce

4cm/1½in fresh root ginger, peeled and very finely sliced

chopped fresh coriander (cilantro), to garnish

### FOR THE STOCK

1 meaty chicken carcass

2 onions, peeled and quartered

4 garlic cloves, crushed

4cm/1½in fresh root ginger, chopped

30ml/2 tbsp *nuoc mam*

30ml/2 tbsp soy sauce

6 black peppercorns

a few sprigs of fresh thyme

sea salt

1 To make the stock, put the chicken carcass into a deep pan. Add all the other stock ingredients except the salt and pour over 2 litres/3½ pints/8 cups of water. Bring the water to the boil, and boil for a few minutes, skim off any foam, then reduce the heat and simmer gently with the lid on for 1½–2 hours. Remove the lid and simmer for a further 30 minutes to reduce the stock. Skim off any fat, season with salt, then strain the stock and measure out 1.5 litres/2½ pints/6¼ cups.

2 Blanch the cabbage leaves in boiling water for about 2 minutes, or until tender. Remove with tongs or a slotted spoon and refresh under cold water. Add the green tops of the spring onions to the boiling water and blanch for a minute, or until tender, then drain and refresh under cold water. Carefully tear each piece into five thin strips and set aside.

3 Squeeze dry the cloud ear mushrooms, then trim and finely chop and mix with the pork, prawns, spring onion whites, chilli, *nuoc mam* and soy sauce. Lay a cabbage leaf flat on a surface and place a teaspoon of the filling about 1cm/½in from the bottom edge. Fold this bottom edge over the filling, and then fold in the sides of the leaf to seal it. Roll all the way to the top of the leaf to form a tight bundle. Wrap a piece of blanched spring onion green around the bundle and tie it so that it holds together. Repeat with the remaining leaves and filling.

4 Bring the stock to the boil in a wok or deep pan. Stir in the finely sliced ginger, then reduce the heat and drop in the cabbage bundles. Bubble very gently over a medium heat for about 20 minutes to ensure that the filling is thoroughly cooked. Serve immediately, ladled into bowls with a sprinkling of fresh coriander leaves.

Nutritional information per portion: Energy 106Kcal/447kJ; Protein 14g; Carbohydrate 9g, of which sugars 1g; Fat 2g, of which saturates 0g; Cholesterol 77mg; Calcium 43mg; Fibre 0.3g; Sodium 1.1g

# Aromatic broth with roast duck, pak choi and egg noodles

Served on its own, this Chinese-inspired soup, *mi vit tim*, makes a delicious autumn or winter meal. In a Vietnamese household, a bowl of whole fresh or marinated chillies might be presented as a fiery side dish to chew on, but I prefer to slice and scatter them over the soup with a sprinkling of herbs. This recipe can be made with chicken stock and leftover duck meat from a roasted duck or by roasting a duck, slicing off the breast and thigh meat for the soup, and then using the meaty carcass to make a stock.

**serves 4**

15ml/1 tbsp vegetable oil

2 shallots, thinly sliced

4cm/1½in fresh root ginger, peeled and sliced

15ml/1 tbsp soy sauce

5ml/1 tsp five-spice powder

10ml/2 tsp sugar

175g/6oz pak choi (bok choy)

450g/1lb fresh egg noodles

350g/12oz roast duck, thinly sliced

sea salt

FOR THE STOCK

1 chicken or duck carcass

2 carrots, peeled and quartered

2 onions, peeled and quartered

4cm/1½in fresh root ginger, peeled and cut into chunks

2 lemon grass stalks, chopped

30ml/2 tbsp *nuoc mam*

15ml/1 tbsp soy sauce

6 black peppercorns

FOR THE GARNISH

4 spring onions (scallions), sliced

1–2 red Serrano chillies, seeded and finely sliced

1 bunch each of coriander (cilantro) and basil, stalks removed, leaves chopped

1 To make the stock, put the chicken or duck carcass into a deep pan. Add all the other stock ingredients and pour in roughly 2.5 litres/4½ pints/10¼ cups water. Bring the water to the boil, and boil for a few minutes, skim off any foam, then reduce the heat and simmer gently with the lid on for 2–3 hours. Remove the lid and continue to simmer for a further 30 minutes to reduce the stock. Skim off any fat, season with salt, then strain the stock. Measure out 2 litres/3½ pints/8 cups.

2 Heat the oil in a wok or deep pan and stir in the shallots and ginger. Add the soy sauce, five-spice powder, sugar and stock and bring to the boil. Season with a little salt, reduce the heat and simmer for 10–15 minutes.

3 Meanwhile, cut the pak choi diagonally into wide strips and blanch in boiling water to soften them. Drain and refresh under cold running water to prevent them cooking any further. Bring a large pan of water to the boil, then add the fresh noodles. Cook for 5 minutes, then drain well.

4 Separate the noodles into four soup bowls, lay some of the pak choi and sliced duck over them, and then ladle over generous amounts of the simmering broth. Garnish with the spring onions, chillies and herbs, and serve immediately.

## using dried noodles

If you can't find fresh egg noodles, you can use dried instead. Soak them in lukewarm water for 20 minutes, then cook, one portion at a time, in a sieve lowered into the boiling water. Use a chopstick to untangle them as they soften.

Nutritional information per portion: Energy 673Kcal/2836kJ; Protein 37g; Carbohydrate 86g, of which sugars 22g; Fat 6g, of which saturates 1g; Cholesterol 81mg; Calcium 4mg; Fibre 0.7g; Sodium 0.7g

# Hot-and-sour fish soup

This unusual tangy soup, *canh chua ca*, can be found throughout South-east Asia – with the balance of hot, sweet and sour flavours varying from Cambodia to Thailand to Vietnam. Chillies provide the heat, tamarind produces the tartness and, in Vietnam, where it is the second most cultivated fruit (banana being the first), the delicious sweetness comes from ripe pineapple.

## serves 4

1 catfish, sea bass or red snapper, about 1kg/2¼lb, filleted
25g/1oz dried squid, soaked in water for 30 minutes
15ml/1 tbsp vegetable oil
2 spring onions (scallions), sliced
2 shallots, sliced
4cm/1½in fresh root ginger, peeled and chopped
2–3 lemon grass stalks, cut into strips and crushed
30ml/2 tbsp tamarind paste
2–3 Thai chillies, seeded and sliced
15ml/1 tbsp sugar
30–45ml/2–3 tbsp *nuoc mam*
225g/8oz fresh pineapple, peeled and diced
3 tomatoes, skinned, seeded and roughly chopped
50g/2oz canned sliced bamboo shoots, drained
1 small bunch of fresh coriander (cilantro), stalks removed, leaves finely chopped
salt and ground black pepper
115g/4oz/½ cup beansprouts and 1 bunch of dill, fronds roughly chopped, to garnish
1 lime, cut into quarters, to serve

FOR THE MARINADE
30ml/2 tbsp *nuoc mam*
2 garlic cloves, finely chopped

1 Cut the fish into bitesize pieces. Reserve the head, tail and bones for the stock. In a bowl, mix together the marinade ingredients and add the fish pieces. Toss until well coated, cover and set aside. Drain and rinse the soaked dried squid.

2 Heat the oil in a deep pan and stir in the spring onions, shallots, ginger, lemon grass and dried squid. Add the reserved fish head, tail and bones, and sauté them gently for a minute or two. Pour in 1.2 litres/2 pints/ 5 cups water and bring to the boil. Reduce the heat and simmer for 30 minutes.

3 Strain the stock into another deep pan and bring the clear broth to the boil. Stir in the tamarind paste, chillies, sugar and *nuoc mam* and simmer for 2–3 minutes. Add the pineapple, tomatoes and bamboo shoots and simmer for a further 2–3 minutes. Finally stir in the fish pieces and the chopped fresh coriander, and cook until the fish turns opaque.

4 Season to taste and ladle the soup into hot bowls. Garnish with beansprouts and dill, and serve with the lime quarters to squeeze over.

### hot and sour

Depending on your mood, or your palate, you can adjust the balance of hot and sour by adding more chilli or tamarind to taste. Enjoyed as a meal in itself, the soup is usually served with plain steamed rice but in Saigon it is served with chunks of fresh baguette, which are perfect for soaking up the spicy, fruity, tangy broth.

Nutritional information per portion: Energy 335Kcal/1415kJ; Protein 44g; Carbohydrate 24g, of which sugars 19g; Fat 7g, of which saturates 1g; Cholesterol 108mg; Calcium 138mg; Fibre 2.3g; Sodium 1.2g

# Crab and asparagus soup with nuoc cham

In this delicious example of a *sup*, the recipe has clearly been adapted from the classic French *asparagus velouté* to produce a meatier version that has more texture, and the Vietnamese stamp of *nuoc cham*. Generally, jars of asparagus preserved in brine are used for this recipe, or fresh asparagus that has been steamed until very soft and tender. It is best to avoid canned asparagus though, because it tends to have a metallic taste.

### serves 4

15ml/1 tbsp vegetable oil

2 shallots, finely chopped

2 garlic cloves, finely chopped

15ml/1 tbsp rice flour or
    cornflour (cornstarch)

225g/8oz/1⅓ cups cooked crab
    meat, chopped into small pieces

450g/1lb preserved asparagus,
    finely chopped or 450g/1lb fresh
    asparagus, trimmed and steamed

salt and ground black pepper

basil and coriander (cilantro) leaves,
    to garnish

*nuoc cham*, to serve

FOR THE STOCK

1 meaty chicken carcass

25g/1oz dried shrimp, soaked in
    water for 30 minutes, rinsed
    and drained

2 onions, peeled and quartered

2 garlic cloves, crushed

15ml/1 tbsp *nuoc mam*

6 black peppercorns

sea salt

1 To make the stock, put the chicken carcass into a deep pan. Add all the other stock ingredients, except the salt, and pour in 2 litres/3½ pints/8 cups water. Bring the water to the boil, and boil for a few minutes, skim off any foam, then reduce the heat and simmer gently with the lid on for 1½–2 hours. Remove the lid and continue to simmer for a further 30 minutes to reduce the stock. Skim off any fat, season with salt, then strain the stock and measure out roughly 1.5 litres/2½ pints/6¼ cups.

2 Heat the oil in a deep pan or wok. Stir in the shallots and garlic, until they begin to colour. Remove from the heat, stir in the flour, and then pour in the stock. Put the pan back over the heat and bring the liquid to the boil, stirring constantly, until smooth.

3 Add the crab meat and asparagus, reduce the heat and leave to simmer for 15–20 minutes. Season to taste with salt and pepper, then ladle the soup into bowls, garnish with fresh basil and coriander leaves, and serve with a splash of *nuoc cham*.

### soup by the sea

In households close to the sea, where large crabs – some as large as 60cm/2ft in diameter – can be found in abundance, this soup may be made using a very generous quantity of fresh crab. If you have a good supply of fresh crabs, you can increase the quantity of crab meat as much as you like, to make a soup that is very rich and filling.

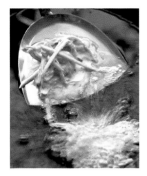

# Food on the go

The Vietnamese are keen snackers. Life is often lived in the streets, so wherever you go there are small restaurants, cafés and makeshift stalls, made out of bamboo, selling or cooking every type of sweet or savoury snack. The southern city of Saigon is abuzz with the sounds and sights of culinary activity, and the streets are so enticingly thick with cooking aromas you could almost bite the air. From the moment the city awakens just before dawn, the stools and tables appear ready for the constant stream of customers.

Pungent spices, such as cinnamon, ginger and star anise, tickle your nose as you walk among the remarkably controlled chaos of sputtering motorbikes, pedestrians dodging traffic, tinkling bicycles with ducks and hens spilling out of baskets, and the cacophony of chattering voices as hoardes of people descend on the food stalls and cafés in overwhelming numbers.

By the middle of the morning, the streets and markets are bustling with activity. Street vendors grill (broil) and steam their food, and the air is thick with the sounds of chopping and hollering, quacking and flapping, and the ordering of noodles, spring rolls and rice cakes steamed in banana leaves. A woman will weave through the crowds bearing a *don ganh*, the rice carrier consisting of a long bamboo pole with a basket at each end. However, she won't be carrying rice in it but rather fresh baguettes or spring rolls, or perhaps even a portable cooker on which she will deftly stir-fry a bowl of delicious noodles. The fruit sellers will also make their way through the crowds, pushing a cart of pineapple, mango or papaya, freshly peeled and kept cool on a bed of ice. In the heat of the day, there's always someone there to press juice from fresh coconuts and sugar cane. All in all, you don't have to look for food in Vietnam – it finds you.

Along the Mekong Delta, some of the markets are conducted on boats. The best known is the floating market Cai Ran, where all the boats converge at dawn. It is a colourful sight, as the boats bob about in the water laden with green bitter melons, long, white radishes, scarlet tomatoes, yellow fruits and heaps of freshly cut herbs. Occasionally, the boats will be pushed along by the quiet skipper wielding a wooden paddle, his face shielded by a wide, conical hat. The atmosphere at these floating markets is one of peacefulness as the sellers hover in the water to chat, while you admire the baskets of produce in the boat. And from time to time, the sound of an outboard motor zips the air as the tea boat chugs around the market answering signals requesting a drink of tea.

*Sizzling crêpes, or* banh xeo, *are one of the most popular street foods in Saigon (right). Pork pâté wrapped in banana leaves (opposite) and deep-fried sweet potato and prawns (top).*

To come back to earth, you just need to wander into one of the countryside village markets where the smells and sights are reminiscent of a busy barnyard. Once again motorbikes and bicycles fight against the crowds and noodle stalls for space. The squawking and cackling of hens and ducks, and other livestock, remind you that the Vietnamese like their ingredients fresh!

One of the first words you are likely to learn in Vietnam is *banh*. There is no direct translation, but it's used loosely to describe street snacks – from spring rolls and crêpes to sandwiches and rice cakes wrapped in banana leaves. You will find them everywhere, piled into baskets, stacked on counters and cooking over charcoal. Sweet or savoury, the one thing *banh* have in common is that they are eaten with the fingers. Look out for the popular southern speciality *banh xeo* (sizzling crêpes) and its counterpart from central Vietnam, *banh khoai* (happy crêpes). Both are light, crispy, crunchy and chewy all at once, filled with minced pork, prawns (shrimp), spring onions (scallions) and beansprouts. It is a sight to behold the pancakes being prepared to order, with the coconut milk batter sizzling in the pan and the magical aromas lifting into the air.

# Grilled shrimp paste on sugar cane skewers

This dish, known as *chao tom* in Vietnam, is a classic. Originally created by the ingenious cooks of the imperial kitchens in Hue, it has become a national treasure. To appreciate its full impact, I prefer simply to grill it and eat it by itself, enjoying every single bite, right down to the sweet, smoky flavours of the sugar cane. *Chao tom* vendors in the streets of Hue, Hanoi and Saigon supply this delicious snack all day long.

**serves 4**

50g/2oz pork fat

7.5ml/1½ tsp vegetable oil

1 onion, finely chopped

2 garlic cloves, crushed

1 egg

15ml/1 tbsp fish sauce

15ml/1 tbsp raw cane or dark brown
   sugar

15ml/1 tbsp cornflour (cornstarch)

350g/12oz raw prawns (shrimp),
   peeled and deveined

a piece of fresh sugar cane, about
   20cm/8in long

salt and ground black pepper

1 Place the pork fat in a pan of boiling water and boil for 2–3 minutes. Drain well and chop using a sharp knife. Set aside.

2 Heat the oil in a heavy pan and stir in the onion and garlic. Just as they begin to colour, remove from the heat and tip them into a bowl. Beat in the egg, fish sauce and sugar, until the sugar has dissolved. Season with a little salt and plenty of black pepper, and then stir in the cornflour.

3 Add the pork fat and prawns to the mixture, and mix well. Transfer to a food processor and process to a slightly lumpy paste, or grind in a mortar using a pestle.

4 Divide the paste into eight portions. Using a strong knife or cleaver, cut the sugar cane in half and then cut each piece into quarters lengthways. Take a piece of sugar cane in your hand and mould a portion of the paste around it, pressing it gently so the edges are sealed. Place the coated sticks on an oiled tray, while you make the remaining skewers in the same way.

5 For the best flavour, cook the shrimp paste skewers over a barbecue for 5–6 minutes, turning them frequently until they are nicely browned all over. Alternatively, cook the skewers under a conventional grill (broiler). Serve immediately.

### fresh sugar cane

Although canned sugar cane can be used for this recipe, it is no substitute for fresh. Fresh sugar cane is often available in African, Caribbean and Asian markets, as well as in some supermarkets. When cooked in the Vietnamese home, this dish is usually served with the traditional accompaniments of salad, rice wrappers and a dipping sauce. The grilled shrimp paste is pulled off the sugar cane, wrapped in a rice paper and dipped in sauce. The stripped sugar cane can then be chewed.

Nutritional information per portion: Energy 159Kcal/668kJ; Protein 18g; Carbohydrate 11g, of which sugars 6g; Fat 5g, of which saturates 1g; Cholesterol 230mg; Calcium 89mg; Fibre 0.6g; Sodium 0.5g

# Grilled prawns with lemon grass

The use of fresh, aromatic lemon grass for grilling, stir-frying or steaming shellfish is a classic feature of Indo-Chinese cooking. Next to every fish and shellfish stall in every market in Vietnam, there is bound to be someone doing just that – cooking up fragrant, citrus-scented snacks for you to eat as you wander around the market. The aromas will entice you to taste, but check what's cooking first, because the Vietnamese also like to cook frogs' legs and snails this way.

**serves 4**

16 king prawns (jumbo shrimp),
  cleaned, with shells intact
120ml/4fl oz/½ cup *nuoc mam*
30ml/2 tbsp sugar
15ml/1 tbsp vegetable
  or sesame oil
3 lemon grass stalks, trimmed
  and finely chopped

1  Using a small sharp knife, carefully slice open each king prawn shell along the back and pull out the black vein, using the point of the knife. Try to keep the rest of the shell intact. Place the deveined prawns in a shallow dish and set aside.

2  Put the *nuoc mam* in a small bowl with the sugar, and beat together until the sugar has dissolved completely. Add the oil and lemon grass and mix well.

3  Pour the marinade over the prawns, using your fingers to rub it all over the prawns and inside the shells too. Cover the dish with clear film (plastic wrap) and chill for at least 4 hours.

4  Cook the prawns on a barbecue or under a conventional grill (broiler) for 2–3 minutes each side. Serve immediately with little bowls of water for rinsing sticky fingers.

**king prawns**

Big, juicy king prawns (jumbo shrimp) are best for this recipe, but you can use smaller ones if the very large king prawns are not available. Other shellfish, such as squid, are also good cooked in this way.

Nutritional information per portion: Energy 174Kcal/726kJ; Protein 13g; Carbohydrate 11g, of which sugars 0g; Fat 9g, of which saturates 1g; Cholesterol 169mg; Calcium 30mg; Fibre 0.3g; Sodium 0.3g

# Fried squid with salt and pepper

Cooking squid couldn't be simpler. Salt and pepper are used to season, and that's it. A great Chinese tradition for all sorts of fish and shellfish, this is a Vietnamese favourite too. Ideal snack and finger food, the tender squid can be served on its own, with noodles or – as it is in the streets of Saigon – with baguette and chillies. Those who like chilli can replace the black pepper with chopped dried chilli or chilli powder. Butterflied prawns or shrimp, with the shells removed, are also delicious cooked in this way.

1 Prepare the squid by pulling the head away from the body. Sever the tentacles from the rest and trim them. Reach inside the body sac and pull out the backbone, then clean the squid inside and out, removing any skin. Rinse well in cold water.

2 Using a sharp knife, slice the squid into rings and pat them dry. Put them on a dish with the tentacles. Combine the salt and pepper with the rice flour or cornflour, tip it on to the squid and toss well, making sure it's evenly coated.

3 Heat the oil in a wok or heavy pan for deep-frying. Cook the squid in batches, until the rings turn crisp and golden. Drain on kitchen paper and serve with lime to squeeze over.

**serves 4**

450g/1lb baby or medium squid

30ml/2 tbsp coarse salt

15ml/1 tbsp ground black pepper

50g/2oz/½ cup rice flour or
  cornflour (cornstarch)

vegetable or sesame oil, for frying

2 limes, halved

Nutritional information per portion: Energy 339Kcal/1405kJ; Protein 14g; Carbohydrate 5g, of which sugars 0g; Fat 29g, of which saturates 4g; Cholesterol 146mg; Calcium 70mg; Fibre 0g; Sodium 1.4g

# Deep-fried sweet potato and prawn patties

This dish, *banh tom*, is a Hanoi speciality. The street sellers in the city and the cafés along the banks of West Lake are well known for their varied and delicious *banh tom*. You can make the patties any size: small for a snack or first course, or large for a main course; simply adjust the amount you spoon on to the spatula before frying. Traditionally, the patties are served with herb and lettuce leaves for wrapping and a sauce for dipping.

**serves 4**

50g/2oz/½ cup plain (all-purpose) flour

50g/2oz/½ cup rice flour

scant 5ml/1 tsp baking powder

10ml/2 tsp sugar

2.5cm/1in fresh root ginger, peeled and grated

2 spring onions (scallions), finely sliced

175g/6oz small fresh prawns (shrimp), peeled and deveined

1 slim sweet potato, about 225g/8oz, peeled and cut into fine matchsticks

vegetable oil, for deep-frying

salt and ground black pepper

chopped fresh coriander (cilantro), to garnish

*nuoc cham* or other dipping sauce, to serve

1 Sift the flours and baking powder into a bowl. Add the sugar and about 2.5ml/½ tsp each of salt and pepper. Gradually stir in 250ml/8fl oz/1 cup water, until thoroughly combined. Add the grated ginger and sliced spring onions and leave to stand for 30 minutes.

2 Add the prawns and sweet potato to the batter and gently fold them in, making sure they are well coated. Heat enough oil for deep-frying in a wok or heavy pan. Place a heaped tablespoon of the mixture on to a metal spatula and pat it down a little. Lower it into the oil, pushing it off the spatula so that it floats in the oil. Fry the patty for 2–3 minutes, turning it over so that it is evenly browned. Drain on kitchen paper. Continue with the rest of the batter, frying the patties in small batches.

3 Arrange the patties on a dish, garnish with coriander, and serve immediately with *nuoc cham* or another dipping sauce of your choice.

### using other vegetables

*Banh tom* made with sweet potato are particularly popular in Hanoi, but they are also very good made with strips of winter melon or courgette (zucchini), beansprouts or bamboo shoots, or finely sliced cabbage leaves. Simply substitute the sweet potato with the vegetable of your choice, add a little chilli, shape into patties and cook as before.

Nutritional information per portion: Energy 276Kcal/1159kJ; Protein 11g; Carbohydrate 35g, of which sugars 6g; Fat 11g, of which saturates 1g; Cholesterol 85mg; Calcium 83mg; Fibre 81g; Sodium 0.2g

# Vietnamese spring rolls

One of the most popular foods throughout Vietnam is the spring roll, which makes an ideal quick snack. They are called *cha gio* in the south and *nem ran* in the north, and their fillings vary from region to region. Freshly fried, straight out of the pan, they are very moreish, especially when dipped in a piquant sauce such as *nuoc cham*. As they are quite fiddly and time-consuming to make, families often prepare large trays of them for special occasions and feasts, serving them with leafy herbs and a table salad. Otherwise, it's easier to eat them in restaurants, or buy them from a spring roll seller in the street.

**makes about 30**

30 dried rice wrappers

vegetable oil, for deep-frying

1 bunch of fresh mint, stalks
   removed, and *nuoc cham*, to serve

FOR THE FILLING

50g/2oz dried bean thread
   (cellophane) noodles, soaked
   in warm water for 20 minutes

25g/1oz dried cloud ear (wood ear)
   mushrooms, soaked in warm water
   for 15 minutes

2 eggs

30ml/2 tbsp *nuoc mam*

2 garlic cloves, crushed

10ml/2 tsp sugar

1 onion, finely chopped

3 spring onions (scallions),
   finely sliced

350g/12oz/1½ cups minced
   (ground) pork

175g/6oz/1¾ cups cooked crab
   meat or raw prawns (shrimp)

salt and ground black pepper

1 To make the filling, squeeze dry the soaked noodles and chop them into small pieces. Squeeze dry the soaked dried cloud ear mushrooms and chop them.

2 Beat the eggs in a bowl. Stir in the *nuoc mam*, garlic and sugar. Add the onion, spring onions, noodles, mushrooms, pork and crab meat or prawns. Season well with salt and ground black pepper.

3 Have ready a damp dishtowel, some clear film (plastic wrap) and a bowl of water. Dip a rice wrapper in the water and place it on the damp towel. Spoon about 15ml/1 tbsp of the spring roll filling on to the side nearest to you, just in from the edge. Fold the nearest edge over the filling, fold over the sides, tucking them in neatly, and then roll the whole wrapper into a tight cylinder. Place the roll on a plate and cover with clear film to keep it moist. Continue making spring rolls in the same way, using the remaining wrappers and filling.

4 Heat the vegetable oil in a wok or heavy pan for deep-frying. Make sure it is hot enough by dropping in a small piece of bread; it should foam and sizzle. Cook the spring rolls in batches, turning them in the oil so that they become golden all over. Drain them on kitchen paper and serve immediately with mint leaves to wrap around them and *nuoc cham* for dipping.

## using beansprouts and fresh herbs

These spring rolls filled with rice noodles are typically Vietnamese, but you can substitute beansprouts for the noodles to create spring rolls more akin to the Chinese version. Fresh mint leaves give these rolls a refreshing bite, but fresh coriander (cilantro), basil or flat-leaf parsley work just as well and give an interesting flavour.

Nutritional information per portion: Energy 63Kcal/236kJ; Protein 2g; Carbohydrate 5g, of which sugars 1g; Fat 4g, of which saturates 1g; Cholesterol 20mg; Calcium 10mg; Fibre 0.3g; Sodium 0.06g

# Saigon sizzling crêpes

French in style, but Vietnamese in flavour, these delightfully crispy, tasty crêpes, made with coconut milk and filled with prawns, mushrooms and beansprouts, are out of this world. The crêpe-makers – from pretty teenage girls to toothless old women – are like mythical sirens of the street. From the moment the batter hits the hot pan, the "sizzling song" begins as they swirl and flip in such hypnotic motion you are magnetically drawn in. These crêpes (*banh xeo*) are Saigon in a mouthful, and it comes as no surprise to learn that they are considered to be powerful aphrodisiacs. Along the same lines, but smaller and less spicy, are the *banh khoai* (happy crêpes) of north and central Vietnam.

## makes 4 large or 8 small
115g/4oz/½ cup minced (ground) pork
15ml/1 tbsp *nuoc mam*
2 garlic cloves, crushed
175g/6oz/⅔ cup button (white) mushrooms, finely sliced
about 60ml/4 tbsp vegetable oil
1 onion, finely sliced
1–2 green or red Thai chillies, seeded and finely sliced
115g/4oz prawns (shrimp), shelled and deveined
225g/8oz/1 cup beansprouts
1 small bunch of fresh coriander (cilantro), stalks removed, leaves roughly chopped
salt and ground black pepper
*nuoc cham*, to serve

### FOR THE BATTER
115g/4oz/1 cup rice flour
10ml/2 tsp ground turmeric
10ml/2 tsp curry powder
5ml/1 tsp sugar
2.5ml/½ tsp salt
300ml/½ pint/1¼ cups canned coconut milk
4 spring onions (scallions), trimmed and finely sliced

1 To make the batter, beat the rice flour, spices, sugar and salt with the coconut milk and 300ml/½ pint/1¼ cups water, until smooth and creamy. Stir in the spring onions and then leave to stand for 30 minutes.
2 In a bowl, mix the pork with the *nuoc mam*, garlic and seasoning and knead well.
3 Lightly sauté the sliced mushrooms in 15ml/1 tbsp of the oil and set aside.
4 Heat 10ml/2 tsp of the oil in a wide, heavy, non-stick pan. Stir in a quarter of the onion and chilli, then add a quarter each of the pork mixture and the prawns. Pour in 150ml/¼ pint/⅔ cup of the batter, swirling the pan so that it spreads over the pork and prawns right to the edges.
5 Pile a quarter of the beansprouts and mushrooms on one side of the crêpe, just in from the middle. Reduce the heat and cover the pan for 2–3 minutes, or until the edges pull away from the sides. Remove the lid and cook the crêpe for another 2 minutes; gently lift up an edge of the crêpe with a spatula to see if it's brown underneath.
6 Once it is nicely browned, scatter some coriander over the empty side of the crêpe and fold it over the beansprouts and mushrooms. Slide the crêpe on to a plate and keep warm while you make the remaining crêpes in the same way. Serve with *nuoc cham* for dipping.

Nutritional information per portion: Energy 379Kcal/1581kJ; Protein 18g; Carbohydrate 37g, of which sugars 9g; Fat 18g, of which saturates 3g; Cholesterol 77mg; Calcium 119mg; Fibre 3.2g; Sodium 0.5g

# Pork pâté in a banana leaf

Having adopted freshly baked baguettes from the French, the Vietnamese also learned how to make pâté to put on them. However, the pâté, *cha lua*, has a Vietnamese twist: it is steamed in banana leaves and has a slightly springy texture and delicate flavour. Baguettes are a common sight alongside the noodles and vegetables in southern markets, and just as frequently spotted are the sandwich carts, displaying halved baguettes smeared with pâté. Another way the Vietnamese eat this pâté is to drizzle it with *nuoc cham* and serve it with a salad. It can also be added to soups and stir-fried dishes, in which it is complemented by fresh herbs and spices.

**serves 6**

45ml/3 tbsp *nuoc mam*

30ml/2 tbsp vegetable or sesame oil

15ml/1 tbsp sugar

10ml/2 tsp five-spice powder

2 shallots, peeled and
  finely chopped

2 garlic cloves, crushed

750g/1lb 10oz/3¼ cups minced
  (ground) pork

25g/1oz/¼ cup potato starch

7.5ml/1½ tsp baking powder

1 banana leaf, trimmed into a strip
  25cm/10in wide

vegetable oil, for brushing

salt and ground black pepper

*nuoc cham* and a baguette
  or salad, to serve

1 In a bowl, beat the *nuoc mam* and oil with the sugar and five-spice powder. Once the sugar has dissolved, stir in the shallots and garlic. Add the minced pork and seasoning, and knead well until thoroughly combined. Cover and chill for 2–3 hours.

2 Knead the mixture again, thumping it down into the bowl to remove any air. Add the potato starch and baking powder and knead until smooth and pasty. Mould the pork mixture into a fat sausage, about 18cm/7in long, and place it on an oiled dish.

3 Lay the banana leaf on a flat surface, brush it with oil, and place the pork sausage across it. Lift up the edge of the leaf nearest to you and fold it over the sausage, tuck in the sides, and roll it up into a tight bundle. Secure the bundle with a piece of string.

4 Fill a wok one-third full with water and balance a bamboo steamer, with its lid on, just above the level of the water. Bring the water to the boil, lift the bamboo lid and place the banana leaf

bundle on the rack, being very careful of any escaping steam. Re-cover and steam for about 45 minutes. Leave the pâté to cool in the leaf, then open it up and cut it into slices. Drizzle with plenty of *nuoc cham*, and serve with a fresh baguette or salad.

### banana leaves

You can find banana leaves in African, Caribbean and Asian markets. To prepare them, trim the leaves to fit the steamer, using a pair of scissors, making sure that there is enough to fold over the pâté. If you cannot find banana leaves, you can use large spring green (collard) leaves, or several Savoy cabbage leaves instead.

Nutritional information per portion: Energy 234Kcal/978kJ; Protein 28g; Carbohydrate 8g, of which sugars 3g; Fat 10g, of which saturates 2g; Cholesterol 79mg; Calcium 46mg; Fibre 0.4g; Sodium 0.7g

# Chilli and honey-cured dried beef

When it comes to ingredients, the Vietnamese will dry almost anything – fish, chillies, mushrooms, snake, herbs, mangoes, pigs' ears and beef are just some of them. Drying is an ancient method of preserving food, which also intensifies the flavour or potency of most ingredients. Some dried goods are destined for stews, soups and medicinal purposes, whereas others are just for chewing on as a snack. You will need a few days to dry the beef in this recipe. If you're lucky this can be done under the sun, otherwise you will need to leave it in the refrigerator.

1 Trim the beef and cut it against the grain into thin, rectangular slices, then set aside.
2 Using a mortar and pestle, grind the lemon grass, garlic and chillies to a paste. Stir in the honey, *nuoc mam* and soy sauce. Put the beef into a bowl, tip in the paste and rub it into the meat. Spread out the meat on a wire rack and place it in the refrigerator, uncovered, for 2 days.
3 Cook the dried beef on the barbecue or under a conventional grill (broiler), and serve it as a snack on its own or with rice wrappers, fresh herbs and a dipping sauce.

**serves 4**

450g/1lb beef sirloin
2 lemon grass stalks, trimmed
   and chopped
2 garlic cloves, chopped
2 dried Serrano chillies, seeded
   and chopped
30–45ml/2–3 tbsp honey
15ml/1 tbsp *nuoc mam*
30ml/2 tbsp soy sauce
rice wrappers, fresh herbs
   and dipping sauce,
   to serve (optional)

Nutritional information per portion: Energy 138Kcal/581kJ; Protein 18g; Carbohydrate 9g, of which sugars 8g; Fat 3g, of which saturates 2g; Cholesterol 38mg; Calcium 7mg; Fibre 0.1g; Sodium 0.4g

# Rice noodles with fresh herbs

*Bun* is the word used to describe the thin, wiry noodles known as rice sticks or rice vermicelli. However, when the Vietnamese talk about a dish called *bun*, they are usually referring to this recipe, which could be described as a noodle salad – simply tossed with crunchy salad vegetables, fresh herbs and sharp flavourings. *Bun* can be served as a light snack on its own, or with stir-fried seafood or chicken as a more complete meal.

1 Peel the cucumber, cut it in half lengthways, remove the seeds, and cut into matchsticks.
2 Add the rice sticks to a pan of boiling water, loosening them gently, and cook for 3–4 minutes, or until white and *al dente*. Drain, rinse under cold water, and drain again.
3 In a bowl, toss the shredded lettuce, beansprouts, cucumber and herbs together. Add the noodles and lime juice and toss together. Drizzle with a little *nuoc mam* or *nuoc cham* for seasoning, and serve immediately.

**making authentic Hanoi *bun***

In the street stalls and cafés of Hanoi, different types of mint, ginger leaves, oregano and thyme provide the herb bedding for this dish, giving it a really distinctive, fragrant flavour.

**serves 4**

half a small cucumber
225g/8oz dried rice sticks (vermicelli)
4–6 lettuce leaves, shredded
115g/4oz/½ cup beansprouts
1 bunch of mixed basil, coriander
   (cilantro), mint and oregano,
   stalks removed, leaves shredded
juice of half a lime
*nuoc mam* or *nuoc cham*, to drizzle

Nutritional information per portion: Energy 221Kcal/926kJ; Protein 4g; Carbohydrate 48g, of which sugars 1g; Fat 0g, of which saturates 0g; Cholesterol 0mg; Calcium 44mg; Fibre 0.8g; Sodium 0.01g

# Singapore noodles

The Vietnamese have put their own particularly delicious stamp on Singapore noodles, which are popular throughout South-east Asia. In Saigon, the noodles are standard street and café food, an ideal snack for anyone feeling a little peckish. At the Singapore noodle stalls, batches of cold, cooked noodles are kept ready to add to the delicious concoction cooking in the wok. At home, you can make this dish with any kind of noodles – egg or rice, fresh or dried.

**serves 4**

30ml/2 tbsp sesame oil

1 onion, finely chopped

3 garlic cloves, finely chopped

3–4 green or red Thai chillies, seeded and finely chopped

4cm/1½in fresh root ginger, peeled and finely chopped

6 spring onions (scallions), finely chopped

1 skinless chicken breast fillet, cut into bitesize strips

90g/3½oz pork, cut into bitesize strips

90g/3½oz prawns (shrimp), shelled

2 tomatoes, skinned, seeded and chopped

30ml/2 tbsp tamarind paste

15ml/1 tbsp *nuoc mam*

juice and rind of 1 lime

10ml/2 tsp sugar

150ml/¼ pint/⅔ cup water or fish stock

225g/8oz fresh rice sticks (vermicelli)

salt and ground black pepper

1 bunch each of fresh basil and mint, stalks removed, leaves shredded, and *nuoc cham*, to serve

1 Heat a wok or heavy pan and add the oil. Stir in the onion, garlic, chillies and ginger, and cook until they begin to colour. Add the spring onions and cook for 1 minute, add the chicken and pork, and cook for 1–2 minutes, then stir in the prawns.

2 Add the tomatoes, followed by the tamarind paste, *nuoc mam*, lime juice and rind, and sugar. Pour in the water or fish stock, and cook gently for 2–3 minutes.

3 Meanwhile, toss the noodles in a pan of boiling water and cook for a few minutes until tender. Drain them and add to the chicken and prawn mixture. Season with salt and ground black pepper and serve immediately, with plenty of basil and mint scattered over the top, and drizzled with spoonfuls of *nuoc cham*.

**different flavours**

There are endless variations of this classic dish – the only key is to keep the sauce dry, cut the meat and fish into small pieces and, most importantly, toss in the noodles at the last minute. The addition of fresh basil and *nuoc cham* lends a distinct Vietnamese flavour but you may also add strips of squid or slices of Chinese sausage to the mixture in the wok.

Nutritional information per portion: Energy 420Kcal/1756kJ; Protein 23g; Carbohydrate 59g, of which sugars 9g; Fat 10g, of which saturates 2g; Cholesterol 86mg; Calcium 119mg; Fibre 1.3g; Sodium 0.5g

Rice and noodles

# Essential grains

In Vietnam, rice is regarded as the staff of life. It plays an important role on the table as well as in the economy and the culture. Vietnam ranks third in world rice export, behind the United States and Thailand, and its valleys and hillside terraces are lushly carpeted with fertile, well-irrigated rice crops. Many varieties of rice are cultivated, all with their own flavour and gluten content, which the Vietnamese can differentiate just by the aroma. Vietnam's principal rice bowls can be found around the Red River in the north and the Mekong Delta.

When buying, the quality and texture of the grain will be discussed at length by the rice cook, who will require a particular rice for the meal that day. Long grain rice will often be used as the springy bed for many fish and meat curries and stews; the short grain is generally used to make the rice porridge, *chao*, while the chalky-white short grain, which is starchy and sticky when cooked, is easier to handle and mould into savoury and sweet snacks, as well as providing extra bulk for vegetarian dishes. Traditionally, rice dishes are prepared by steaming, stir-frying or cooking the grain until it resembles porridge. However, rice is not just a staple grain, eaten on its own or as an accompaniment to a main dish; it is also used to make vinegar and wine, and it is indispensable when ground into flour to make the French-style baguettes and sizzling crêpes, the ubiquitous, paper-thin wrappers for spring rolls, and the dried and fresh noodles.

The dried rice wrappers, *banh trang*, are unique to Vietnamese cuisine. They are shaped in triangles or rounds and dried in the open air on bamboo mats, which leave a distinctive criss-cross pattern on the brittle wrappers. When reconstituted in water, these wrappers are used for making the fried Vietnamese spring rolls, *cha gio*, and the light summer rolls, *goi cuon*. They are also put on the table to be used as wrappings for salads, meatballs, grilled meats and stir-fried dishes. Wrapping tasty morsels and dipping them in sauce is a typical Vietnamese way of enjoying a meal. In addition to the dried wrappers, there is a fresh rice wrapper, *banh uot*, which is used exclusively for wrapping minced meats.

The everyday noodles in Vietnam can be divided into three main types. *Bun*, which are long and thin, similar to Italian vermicelli and called rice sticks, are used in soups and side-dishes, and as a wrapping for meat and seafood. *Banh pho*, which are also called rice sticks, are flatter, thicker and sturdier, and ideal for substantial soups, such as *pho*, and stir-fries. The fine *banh hoi*, which resemble angel-hair pasta, are primarily used in thin broths.

*Vietnamese sticky rice, called* xoi nep*, requires a long soak in water before being cooked in a bamboo steamer (right). Bamboo-steamed sticky rice (opposite) and long-grain rice (top).*

In addition to the common rice noodles, the Vietnamese also use both wheat and egg noodles, which have been adopted from the Chinese. Less common noodles include *banh cuon*, a kind of Vietnamese ravioli filled with minced pork and cloud ear (wood ear) mushrooms, which are usually tossed in oil and then dipped in the ever-favourite *nuoc cham*; Shanghai egg noodles, called *mi* in Vietnamese but often referred to as Cambodian-style noodles, which are used in stir-fries of Chinese origin; and the Chinese *mien*, bean thread or cellophane noodles, made from mung beans.

Noodles are eaten at all hours of the day: in soup for breakfast, stir-fried for a quick snack, or more elaborately in a main dish, which often appears soup-like to a Western palate. The most common type of restaurant in Vietnam is the rice and noodle shop and these two ingredients make the base of almost every dish, either as an accompaniment or as an essential ingredient within it.

# Steamed rice

Long grain rice is the most frequently eaten grain in Vietnam – freshly steamed and served at almost every meal. If the main dish doesn't include noodles, then a bowl of steamed rice – *com* – or rice wrappers will provide the starch for the meal. Steamed rice forms the main part of the daily diet for many poorer families. A variety of long grain rice is available in Asian markets but, for fragrance, jasmine rice is delicious and easily available. The measured quantity of rice grains doubles when the rice is cooked.

**serves 4**

225g/8oz/generous 1 cup long grain
  rice, rinsed and drained
a pinch of salt

1 Put the rice into a heavy pan or clay pot. Add about 600ml/1 pint/2½ cups water to cover the rice by 2.5cm/1in. Add the salt, and then bring the water to the boil.
2 Reduce the heat, cover the pan and cook gently for about 20 minutes, or until all the water has been absorbed. Remove the pan from the heat and leave to steam, still covered, for a further 5–10 minutes.
3 To serve, simply fluff up with a fork.

Nutritional information per portion: Energy 203Kcal/864kJ; Protein 4g; Carbohydrate 49g, of which sugars 0g; Fat 1g, of which saturates 0g; Cholesterol 0mg; Calcium 2mg; Fibre 0.3g; Sodium 0g

# Bamboo-steamed sticky rice

Vietnamese sticky rice, or glutinous rice, called *xoi nep*, requires a long soak in water before being cooked in a bamboo steamer. It is used for savoury and sweet rice cakes, such as *banh chung* and *Hue com sen*. It is enjoyed as a sweet, filling snack with sugar and coconut milk and, as it is fairly bulky, it is also served with dipping sauces, light dishes and vegetarian meals. Sticky rice is available in Chinese and Asian stores, as well as some supermarkets. The measured quantity of rice grains doubles when cooked.

1 Put the rice into a large bowl and fill the bowl with cold water. Leave the rice to soak for at least 6 hours, then drain, rinse thoroughly, and drain again.

2 Fill a wok or heavy pan one-third full with water. Place a bamboo steamer, with the lid on, over the wok or pan and bring the water to the boil. Uncover the steamer and place a dampened piece of muslin (cheesecloth) over the rack. Tip the rice into the middle and spread it out a little. Fold the muslin over the rice, cover and steam for about 25 minutes until the rice is tender but firm.

**serves 4**
350g/12oz/1¾ **cups sticky rice**

Nutritional information per portion: Energy 314Kcal/1314kJ; Protein 7g; Carbohydrate 66g, of which sugars 0g; Fat 1g, of which saturates 0g; Cholesterol 0mg; Calcium 14mg; Fibre 0g; Sodium 0g

# Sticky rice cakes filled with pork and lotus seeds

In the old imperial city of Hue, this traditional dish, *Hue com sen*, is presented like a beautiful woman, dressed in a lotus leaf and garnished with a fresh lotus flower. For celebrations over New Year, *Tet*, there is a similar dish called *banh chung*, which contains mung beans instead of lotus seeds. In southern Vietnam, banana leaves are used to make these parcels, and they make the perfect substitute if you can't find lotus leaves. Banana leaves are available in most Asian markets, and lotus seeds can be found in Chinese stores. Serve the rice cakes with a salad and dipping sauce.

**makes 2 cakes**

15ml/1 tbsp vegetable oil

2 garlic cloves, chopped

225g/8oz lean pork, cut into
  bitesize chunks

30ml/2 tbsp *nuoc mam*

2.5ml/½ tsp sugar

10ml/2 tsp ground black pepper

115g/4oz lotus seeds, soaked
  for 6 hours and drained

2 lotus or banana leaves, trimmed
  and cut into 25cm/10in squares

500g/1¼lb/5 cups cooked
  sticky rice

salt

1 Heat the oil in a heavy pan. Stir in the garlic, until it begins to colour, then add the pork, *nuoc mam*, sugar and pepper. Cover and cook over a low heat for about 45 minutes, or until the pork is tender. Leave to cool.

2 Meanwhile, bring a pan of salted water to the boil. Reduce the heat and add the prepared lotus seeds. Allow them to cook for about 10 minutes, or until they are tender, then drain, pat dry and leave to cool.

3 Using your fingers, shred the cooked pork and place beside the lotus seeds. Lay a lotus leaf or banana leaf on a flat surface and place a quarter of the cooked sticky rice in the middle of the leaf. Flatten the centre of the rice mound slightly and then scatter with half the shredded pork and half the lotus seeds.

4 Drizzle some of the cooking juices from the pork over the top. Place another quarter of the rice on top, moulding and patting it with your fingers to make sure the pork and lotus seeds are enclosed like a little cake. Fold the leaf edge nearest to you over the rice, tuck in the sides, and fold the whole packet over to form a tight, square bundle. Tie it with string to secure it and set aside. Repeat with the second leaf and the remaining ingredients.

5 Fill a wok one-third full of water. Place a double-tiered bamboo steamer, with its lid on, on top. Bring the water to the boil, lift the bamboo lid and place a rice cake on the rack in each tier. Cover and steam for about 45 minutes. Carefully open up the parcels and serve with a salad and dipping sauce.

Nutritional information per portion: Energy 736Kcal/3071kJ; Protein 42g; Carbohydrate 52g, of which sugars 2g; Fat 41g, of which saturates 5g; Cholesterol 1mg; Calcium 107mg; Fibre 3.7g; Sodium 0.7g

# Saigon southern-spiced chilli rice with turmeric and coriander

Although plain steamed rice is served at almost every meal, many southern families like to sneak in a little spice too. A burst of chilli for fire, turmeric for colour, and coriander its cooling flavour, are all that's needed. This rice goes particularly well with grilled and stir-fried fish and shellfish dishes, but you can serve it as an alternative to plain rice.If you like your rice extra hot and spicy, add another chilli.

**serves 4**

15ml/1 tbsp vegetable oil
  or sesame oil

2–3 green or red Thai chillies,
  seeded and finely chopped

2 garlic cloves, finely chopped

2.5cm/1in fresh root ginger,
  finely chopped

5ml/1 tsp sugar

10–15ml/2–3 tsp ground turmeric

225g/8oz/generous 1 cup long
  grain rice

30ml/2 tbsp *nuoc mam*

600ml/1 pint/2½ cups water,
  or fish or chicken stock

1 bunch of fresh coriander
  (cilantro), stalks removed, leaves
  finely chopped

salt and ground black pepper

1 Heat the oil in a heavy pan. Stir in the chillies, garlic and ginger with the sugar. As they begin to colour, stir in the turmeric. Add the rice, coating it in the turmeric and flavourings, then pour in the *nuoc mam* and the water or stock – the liquid should sit about 2.5cm/1in above the rice.

2 Season with salt and pepper and bring the liquid to the boil. Reduce the heat, cover and simmer for about 25 minutes, or until the water has been absorbed. Remove from the heat and leave the rice to steam for a further 10 minutes.

3 Tip the rice on to a serving dish. Add some of the coriander and lightly toss together using a fork. Garnish with the remaining coriander.

Nutritional information per portion: Energy 252Kcal/1066kJ; Protein 5g; Carbohydrate 51g, of which sugars 1g; Fat 5g, of which saturates 1g; Cholesterol 0mg; Calcium 24mg, ᵁre 0.3g; Sodium 0.5g

# Stir-fried rice with Chinese sausage

Traditional Vietnamese stir-fried rice includes cured Chinese pork sausage, or thin strips of pork combined with prawns or crab. Prepared this way, the dish can be eaten as a snack, or as part of the meal with grilled and roasted meats accompanied by a vegetable dish or salad. The rice used in these stir-fries is usually made the day before and added cold to the dish. If you prefer, you can drizzle sweet, sour or hot *nuoc cham* dipping sauce over the rice instead of the *nuoc mam*.

**serves 4**

25g/1oz dried cloud ear (wood ear)
   mushrooms, soaked for 20 minutes

15ml/1 tbsp vegetable or sesame oil

1 onion, sliced

2 green or red Thai chillies, seeded
   and finely chopped

2 Chinese sausages (15cm/6in long),
   each sliced into 10 pieces

175g/6oz prawns (shrimp), shelled
   and deveined

30ml/2 tbsp *nuoc mam*, plus extra
   for drizzling

10ml/2 tsp five-spice powder

1 bunch of fresh coriander (cilantro),
   stalks removed, leaves
   finely chopped

450g/1lb/4 cups cold steamed rice

ground black pepper

1 Drain the soaked cloud ear mushrooms and cut them into strips. Heat a wok or heavy pan and add the oil. Add the onion and chillies. Fry until they begin to colour, then stir in the mushrooms.

2 Add the sausage slices, moving them around the wok or pan until they begin to brown. Add the prawns and move them around until they turn opaque. Stir in the *nuoc mam*, the five-spice powder and 30ml/2 tbsp of the coriander.

3 Season well with pepper, then quickly add the rice, making sure it doesn't stick to the pan. As soon as the rice is heated through, sprinkle with the remainder of the coriander and serve with *nuoc mam* to drizzle over it.

Nutritional information per portio... ..nergy 398Kcal/1673kJ; Protein 19g; Carbohydrate 44g, of which sugars 4g; Fat 18g, of which saturates 5g; Cholesterol 116mg; Calcium 158mg; Fibre 2g; Sodium 0.8g

# Fragrant rice with chicken, mint and nuoc cham

From the north of Vietnam, where fresh herbs play an important role in the cuisine, this refreshing dish can be served very simply, drizzled with *nuoc cham*, or as part of a celebratory meal that might include fish or chicken, either grilled or roasted whole, and accompanied by pickles and a table salad.

**serves 4**

350g/12oz/1¾ cups long grain rice, rinsed and drained

2–3 shallots, halved and finely sliced

1 bunch of fresh mint, stalks removed, leaves finely shredded

2 spring onions (scallions), finely sliced, to garnish

*nuoc cham*, to serve

FOR THE STOCK

2 meaty chicken legs

1 onion, peeled and quartered

4cm/1½in fresh root ginger, peeled and coarsely chopped

15ml/1 tbsp *nuoc mam*

3 black peppercorns

1 bunch of fresh mint

sea salt

1 To make the stock, put the chicken legs into a deep pan. Add all the other ingredients, except the salt, and pour in 1 litre/1¾ pints/ 4 cups water. Bring the water to the boil, skim off any foam, then reduce the heat and simmer gently with the lid on for 1 hour. Remove the lid, increase the heat and simmer for a further 30 minutes to reduce the stock. Skim off any fat, strain the stock and season with salt. Measure 750ml/1¼ pints/3 cups stock. Remove the chicken meat from the bone and shred.

2 Put the rice in a heavy pan and stir in the stock. When the rice settles, check that the stock sits roughly 2.5cm/1in above the rice; if not, top it up. Bring the liquid to the boil, cover the pan and cook for about 25 minutes, or until all the water has been absorbed.

3 Remove the pan from the heat and, using a fork, add the shredded chicken, shallots and most of the mint. Cover the pan again and leave the flavours to mingle for 10 minutes. Tip the rice into bowls, or on to a serving dish, garnish with the remaining mint and the spring onions, and serve with *nuoc cham*.

### making a meal of it

To serve this dish as a meal on its own, stir-fry strips of pork, slices of Chinese sausage and a handful of prawns (shrimp) and toss into the rice along with the shredded chicken.

Nutritional information per portion: Energy 370Kcal/1569kJ; Protein 12g; Carbohydrate 79g, of which sugars 1g; Fat 3g, of which saturates 0g; Cholesterol 26mg; Calcium 41mg; Fibre 0.8g; Sodium 0.2g

# Fresh rice noodles

A variety of dried noodles is available in Asian stores and supermarkets, but fresh ones are quite different and not that difficult to make. The freshly-made noodle sheets can be served as a snack, drenched in sugar or honey, or dipped into a savoury sauce of your choice. Otherwise, cut them into wide strips and gently stir-fry them with garlic, ginger, chillies and *nuoc mam* or soy sauce.

**serves 4**

225g/8oz/2 cups rice flour

600ml/1 pint/2 ½ cups water

a pinch of salt

15ml/1 tbsp vegetable oil,
   plus extra for brushing

slivers of red chilli and fresh root
   ginger, and fresh coriander
   (cilantro) leaves, to garnish
   (optional)

1 Place the flour in a bowl and stir in some of the water to form a paste. Pour in the rest of the water, beating it to make a lump-free batter. Add the salt and oil and leave it to stand for 15 minutes.

2 Meanwhile, fill a wide pan with water. Cut a piece of smooth cotton cloth a little larger than the diameter of the pan. Stretch it over the top of the pan, pulling the edges tautly down over the sides, then wind a piece of string around the edge, to secure. Using a sharp knife, make three small slits, about 2.5cm/1in from the edge of the cloth, at regular intervals.

3 Bring the water to the boil. Stir the batter and ladle 30–45ml/2–3 tbsp on to the cloth, swirling it to form a 13–15cm/5–6in wide circle. Cover with a domed lid, such as a wok lid, and steam for 1 minute, or until the noodle sheet is translucent.

4 Carefully insert a spatula or knife under the noodle sheet and prise it off the cloth. (If it doesn't peel off easily, you may need to steam it a little longer.) Transfer the noodle sheet to a lightly oiled baking tray, brush lightly with oil, and cook the remaining batter in the same way. From time to time, you may need to top up the water through one of the slits and tighten the cloth again.

Nutritional information per portion: Energy 251Kcal/1046kJ; Protein 4g; Carbohydrate 45g, of which sugars 0g; Fat 5g, of which saturates 1g; Cholesterol 0mg; Calcium 24mg; Fibre 1.1g; Sodium 0.2g

# Noodles with crab and cloud ear mushrooms

This is a dish of contrasting flavours, textures and colours, and in Vietnam it is cooked with skill and dexterity. While one hand gently turns the noodles in the pan, the other takes chunks of fresh crab meat and drops them into the steaming wok to seal. When you watch the expert cooks who specialize in this dish, *mien xao cua*, they make it look like an art form. Here the crab meat is cooked separately to make it easier for the uninitiated.

**serves 4**

25g/1oz dried cloud ear (wood ear) mushrooms, soaked in warm water for 20 minutes

115g/4oz dried bean thread (cellophane) noodles, soaked in warm water for 20 minutes

30ml/2 tbsp vegetable or sesame oil

3 shallots, halved and thinly sliced

2 garlic cloves, crushed

2 green or red Thai chillies, seeded and sliced

1 carrot, peeled and cut into thin diagonal rounds

5ml/1 tsp sugar

45ml/3 tbsp oyster sauce

15ml/1 tbsp soy sauce

400ml/14fl oz/1²/₃ cups water or chicken stock

225g/8oz fresh, raw crab meat, cut into bitesize chunks

ground black pepper

fresh coriander (cilantro) leaves, to garnish

1 Remove the centres from the soaked wood ear mushrooms and cut the mushrooms in half. Drain the soaked noodles and cut them into 30cm/12in pieces.

2 Heat a wok or heavy pan and add 15ml/1 tbsp of the oil. Stir in the shallots, garlic and chillies, and cook until fragrant. Add the carrot rounds and cook for 1 minute, then add the mushrooms. Stir in the sugar with the oyster and soy sauces, followed by the bean thread noodles. Pour in the water or stock, cover the wok or pan and cook for about 5 minutes, or until the noodles are soft and have absorbed most of the sauce.

3 Meanwhile, heat the remaining oil in a heavy pan. Add the crab meat and cook until it is nicely pink and tender. Season well with black pepper. Arrange the noodles and crab meat on a serving dish and garnish with coriander.

Nutritional information per portion: Energy 292Kcal/1224kJ; Protein 16g; Carbohydrate 30g, of which sugars 5g; Fat 13g, of which saturates 2g; Cholesterol 36mg; Calcium 29mg; Fibre 2.5g; Sodium 1g

# Fried noodles with spicy peanut saté, beef and fragrant herbs

If you like chillies and peanuts, this delicious dish makes the perfect choice. You can add as much saté as you like, but remember – it's fiery. The stringy rice sticks are fiddly to stir-fry as they have a tendency to cling to one another, so work quickly and lubricate them with a little extra oil. This dish is usually served with a table salad or pickles.

## serves 4

15–30ml/1–2 tbsp vegetable oil

300g/11oz beef sirloin, cut against the grain into thin slices

225g/8oz dried rice sticks (vermicelli), soaked in warm water for 20 minutes

225g/8oz/1 cup beansprouts

5–10ml/1–2 tsp *nuoc mam*

1 small bunch each of fresh basil and mint, stalks removed, leaves shredded, to garnish

### FOR THE SATÉ

4 dried Serrano chillies, seeded

60ml/4 tbsp groundnut (peanut) or vegetable oil

4–5 garlic cloves, crushed

5–10ml/1–2 tsp curry powder

40g/1½oz/⅓ cup roasted peanuts, finely ground

1 To make the saté, grind the Serrano chillies in a mortar with a pestle. Heat the oil in a heavy pan and stir in the garlic until it begins to colour. Add the chillies, curry powder and the peanuts and stir over a gentle heat, until the mixture forms a paste. Remove the pan from the heat and leave the mixture to cool.

2 Heat a wok or heavy pan, and pour in 15ml/1 tbsp of the oil. Add the sliced beef and cook for 1–2 minutes, and stir in 7.5ml/1½ tsp of the spicy peanut saté. Tip the beef on to a clean plate and set aside while you prepare the noodles.

3 Drain the rice sticks. Add 7.5ml/1½ tsp oil to the wok and add 15ml/1 tbsp saté. Quickly toss the noodles, until they are evenly coated in the sauce (add more oil if they stick together) and cook for 4–5 minutes, or until tender. Toss in the beef for 1 minute, then add the beansprouts with the *nuoc mam*. Tip the noodles on to a serving dish and sprinkle with the basil and mint.

### South-east Asian links

Although it is quite similar to *pad Thai*, one of the national noodle dishes of Thailand, the addition of *nuoc mam*, basil and mint give this fragrant dish a distinctly Vietnamese flavour. There are many similar versions throughout South-east Asia, made with prawns (shrimp), pork and chicken.

Nutritional information per portion: Energy 603Kcal/2507kJ; Protein 26g; Carbohydrate 52g, of which sugars 2g; Fat 32g, of which saturates 6g; Cholesterol 38mg; Calcium 73mg; Fibre 2.2g; Sodium 0.2g

# Crispy egg noodle pancake with prawns, scallops and squid

In dishes of Chinese origin, egg noodles are used instead of rice noodles. For this popular dish, the Vietnamese prefer to use thin Shanghai-style noodles, which are available only in Chinese and Asian markets, but fortunately it does work with other varieties of egg noodle too. Serve with a simple salad or pickled vegetables.

**serves 4**

225g/8oz fresh egg noodles

45ml/3 tbsp vegetable oil,
 plus extra for brushing

FOR THE SEAFOOD

15–30ml/1–2 tbsp vegetable oil

4cm/1½in fresh root ginger, peeled
 and cut into matchsticks

4 spring onions (scallions), trimmed
 and cut into bitesize pieces

1 carrot, peeled and cut into thin,
 diagonal slices

8 scallops (halved if large)

8 baby squid, cut in half lengthways

8 tiger prawns (shrimp), shelled
 and deveined

30ml/2 tbsp *nuoc mam*

45ml/3 tbsp soy sauce

5ml/1 tsp sugar

ground black pepper

fresh coriander (cilantro) leaves,
 to garnish

*nuoc cham*, to serve

1 Bring a large pan of water to the boil. Drop in the noodles, untangling them with chopsticks or a fork. Cook for about 5 minutes, or until tender. Drain thoroughly and spread the noodles out into a wide, thick pancake on an oiled plate. Leave to dry out a little, so that the pancake holds its shape.

2 Heat 30ml/2 tbsp of the oil in a non-stick, heavy pan. Carefully slide the noodle pancake off the plate into the pan and cook over a medium heat until it is crisp and golden underneath. Add a little extra oil to the pan, flip the noodle pancake over and crisp the other side too.

3 While the noodle pancake is cooking, heat a wok or heavy pan and add the oil. Stir in the ginger and spring onions, and cook until they become fragrant. Add the carrot slices, tossing them in the wok, for 1–2 minutes.

4 Add the scallops, squid and prawns, moving them around the wok, so that they sear while cooking. Stir in the *nuoc mam*, soy sauce and sugar and season well with black pepper.

5 Transfer the crispy noodle pancake to a serving dish and tip the seafood on top. Garnish with coriander and serve immediately. To eat, break off pieces of the seafood-covered noodle pancake and drizzle with *nuoc cham*.

### cleaning squid

You can usually ask your fishmonger to prepare the squid, but to prepare squid yourself, get a firm hold of the head and pull it from the body. Reach down inside the body sac and pull out the transparent back bone, as well as any stringy parts. Rinse the body sac inside and out and pat dry. Cut the tentacles off above the eyes and add to the pile of squid you're going to cook. Discard everything else.

Fish and shellfish

# Fresh and dried fish

All along the coastline that runs down the length of Vietnam's eastern shores are open markets with the day's catch of crabs, plump prawns (shrimp), sea bass, mackerel and tuna. Anyone can fish from their boats and sell or eat their catch. Inland there are many rivers – the three principal ones being the Red River in the north, the Perfume River in the centre and the mighty Mekong River in the south, all of which yield great numbers of carp, catfish and eel. The rivers are as busy as the coast with fish markets and wooden boats, *thuyen thung*, which resemble halved coconut shells bobbing in the water.

Using the ancient Chinese methods of fishing with a net and bamboo poles, the Vietnamese excel in their fishing skills both for pleasure and to make ends meet. They even fish in the rice paddies where large breeding ponds for carp, catfish, freshwater prawns and crab have been dug out. In Vietnam, fish and shellfish form part of the daily diet, and such is the passion for them that the national condiment, *nuoc mam*, is a fish sauce made from fermented *ca com* – tiny, translucent fish that resemble silver anchovies. Famous for its *nuoc mam* is the paradisaic island of Phu Quoc in the Gulf of Thailand, where the sight of the deserted, pearly-white beaches and tall, shady palm trees is breath-taking until the intense smell from the pungent fermented fish sauce quite literally takes your breath away.

When cooking fish in Vietnam, only the freshest produce is used. It is sold live, at reasonable prices, in the markets and restaurants and is often bought minutes before going into the pot. This is partly due to the lack of refrigeration in most homes, but also because the Vietnamese appreciate the delicate, sweet flesh of fish and shellfish plucked straight out of the water. To enhance the flavour and texture, many recipes call for a simple infusion with herbs, or steaming with ginger and lemon grass, rather than masking the natural taste with too many spices or strong condiments. One tasty example is the popular *tom nuong xa* – grilled king prawns (jumbo shrimp) with lemon grass – which is easy to prepare at home. The more complex dishes are reserved for special family gatherings or enjoyed when dining out. Usually chunks of fish are stir-fried with herbs, while the larger steaks might be braised with a caramel sauce or steamed in coconut milk or beer. Fish cakes and dumplings are popular too, made with the flaked flesh of fish or pounded shellfish, and they are added to noodle soups or stir-fried to accompany crispy egg noodles. But most of all, the Vietnamese prefer to steam their fish whole because it signifies prosperity; the head is considered a delicacy, believed to bring good luck.

*One of Vietnam's most common fish, fresh baby squid are tender and sweet, and can be cooked in many different ways (right). Baked stuffed crab shells (opposite) and raw tiger prawns (top).*

With such an abundance of fish, methods of preserving it have had to evolve. Hanging the larger fish up to dry, or salting them, is practised throughout Vietnam, as is pickling the smaller varieties. Prawns and squid are so common that they are often salted and dried to be used in dishes and stocks as a seasoning, or to be eaten as a snack. Scallops, clams, crabs and lobsters are less common, but equally as popular. Snails also come into this category, as many are water-dwellers, and are cooked in similar ways. For a daily snack or light meal, shellfish is generally stir-fried or grilled with ginger, chillies and *nuoc mam* or soy sauce and fresh herbs. One of the most basic curries, especially among fishermen, is prawn and cauliflower curry with fenugreek, coconut and lime – a delicious dish from the southern coast of Vietnam that is simple and quick to make, and usually served with noodles or chunks of fresh bread to mop up the tasty sauce. It is often eaten from a communal bowl or from the wok itself. Other popular combinations include prawns with butternut squash, pumpkin or winter melon.

# Hanoi fried fish with dill

The north of Vietnam is well known for its use of pungent herbs, so much so that a dish of the ever-popular noodles can be served plain, dressed only with coriander and basil. There are many herbs that are indigenous to this northern region and virtually impossible to find outside Vietnam, but one herb that is easily available and used in many northern-style fish dishes is dill. In this classic dish from Hanoi, *cha ca Hanoi*, the dill is just as important as the fish and they complement each other beautifully. A simple accompaniment of plain rice or noodles is all that is needed to make an impressive meal.

**serves 4**

75g/3oz/²⁄₃ cup rice flour

7.5ml/1½ tsp ground turmeric

500g/1¼lb white fish fillets, such
    as cod skinned and cut into
    bitesize chunks

vegetable oil, for deep-frying

1 large bunch fresh dill

15ml/1 tbsp groundnut (peanut) oil

30ml/2 tbsp roasted peanuts

4 spring onions (scallions), cut into
    bitesize pieces

1 small bunch of fresh basil, stalks
    removed, leaves chopped

1 small bunch of fresh coriander
    (cilantro), stalks removed

1 lime, cut into quarters, and *nuoc
    cham*, to serve

1 Mix the flour with the turmeric and toss the fish chunks in it until well coated. Heat the oil in a wok or heavy pan and cook the fish in batches until crisp and golden. Drain on kitchen paper.

2 Scatter some of the dill fronds on a serving dish, arrange the fish on top and keep warm. Chop some of the remaining dill fronds and set aside for the garnish.

3 Heat the groundnut oil in a small pan or wok. Stir in the peanuts and cook for 1 minute, then add the spring onions, the remaining dill fronds, basil and coriander. Stir-fry for no more than 30 seconds, then spoon the herbs and peanuts over the fish. Garnish with the chopped dill and serve with lime wedges and *nuoc cham* to drizzle over the top.

**Cha Ca Street**

There is a street in Hanoi called Cha Ca Street, where all the restaurants specialize in this dish. The most famous is Cha Ca La Vong, a tiny restaurant that has been owned by the same family for generations and which claims to have first popularized *cha ca*. This recipe usually uses the local Red River fish, carp and catfish, and is served with piquant dipping sauces such as *mam tong tom* made with pineapple and dried shrimp, or *nuoc cham*.

Nutritional information per portion: Energy 350Kcal/1458kJ; Protein 27g; Carbohydrate 17g, of which sugars 1g; Fat 19g, of which saturates 3g; Cholesterol 85mg; Calcium 112mg; Fibre 1.2g; Sodium 0.2g

# Sea bass steamed in coconut milk with ginger, cashew nuts and basil

This is a delicious recipe for any whole white fish, such as sea bass or cod, or for large chunks of trout or salmon. You will need a steamer large enough to fit the whole fish or, if using fish chunks, you can use a smaller steamer and fit the fish around the base. The recipe also works well in the oven – simply place the fish, tucked in foil, on a baking tray and bake. Serve this dish with plain or sticky rice or a Vietnamese vegetable salad.

**serves 4**

200ml/7fl oz coconut milk

10ml/2 tsp raw cane or muscovado (molasses) sugar

about 15ml/1 tbsp sesame or vegetable oil

2 garlic cloves, finely chopped

1 red Thai chilli, seeded and finely chopped

4cm/1½in ginger, peeled and grated

750g/1lb 10oz sea bass, gutted and skinned on one side

1 star anise, ground

1 bunch of fresh basil, stalks removed

30ml/2 tbsp cashew nuts

sea salt and ground black pepper

1 Heat the coconut milk with the sugar in a small pan, stirring until the sugar dissolves, then remove from the heat. Add the oil to a small frying pan and stir in the garlic, chilli and ginger. Cook until they begin to brown, then add the mixture to the coconut milk and mix well to combine.

2 Place the fish, skin side down, on a wide piece of foil and tuck up the sides to form a boat-shaped container. Using a sharp knife, cut several diagonal slashes into the flesh on the top and rub with the ground star anise. Season with salt and pepper and spoon the coconut milk over the top.

3 Scatter about half the basil leaves over the top of the fish and pull the sides of the foil over the top, so that it is almost enclosed (like a canoe). Gently lay the foil packet in a steamer. Cover the steamer, bring the water to the boil, then reduce the heat and simmer for 20–25 minutes, or until just cooked.

4 Meanwhile, roast the cashew nuts in the small frying pan, adding a little extra oil if necessary. Drain the nuts on kitchen paper, then grind them to crumbs. When the fish is cooked, lift it out of the foil and transfer it to a serving dish. Spoon the cooking juices over, sprinkle with the cashew nut crumbs and garnish with the remaining basil leaves. Serve immediately.

**using pork or beef**

This traditional recipe also works well with loin of pork or fillet of beef. Simply slash the cuts of meat in several places and follow the method above. Once wrapped in foil, place the package on a baking tray and bake in a medium oven.

Nutritional information per portion: Energy 235Kcal/983kJ; Protein 26g; Carbohydrate 8g, of which sugars 6g; Fat 11g, of which saturates 2g; Cholesterol 100mg; Calcium 217mg; Fibre 0.3g; Sodium 0.3g

# Spicy pan-seared tuna with cucumber, garlic and ginger

This popular dish, which can be found all over Vietnam in restaurants or at food stalls, is made with many types of thick-fleshed fish. Tuna is particularly suitable because it is delicious pan-seared and served a little rare.

serves 4

1 small cucumber

10ml/2 tsp sesame oil

2 garlic cloves, bashed

4 tuna steaks

FOR THE DRESSING

4cm/1½in fresh root ginger,
   peeled and roughly chopped

1 garlic clove, roughly chopped

2 green Thai chillies, seeded
   and roughly chopped

45ml/3 tbsp raw cane sugar

45ml/3 tbsp *nuoc mam*

juice of 1 lime

60ml/4 tbsp water

1 To make the dressing, grind the ginger, garlic and chillies to a pulp with the sugar, using a mortar and pestle. Stir in the *nuoc mam*, lime juice and water, and mix well. Leave the dressing to stand for 15 minutes.

2 Cut the cucumber in half lengthways and remove the seeds. Cut the flesh into long, thin strips, using a mandolin if you have one. Toss the cucumber in the dressing and leave to soak for at least 15 minutes.

3 Wipe a heavy pan with the oil and rub the garlic around it. Heat the pan and add the tuna steaks. Sear for a few minutes on both sides, so that the outside is slightly charred but the inside is still rare. Lift the steaks on to a warm serving dish. Using tongs or chopsticks, lift the cucumber strips out of the dressing and arrange them around the steaks. Drizzle the dressing over the tuna, and serve immediately.

Nutritional information per portion: Energy 262Kcal/1103kJ; Protein 31g; Carbohydrate 16g, of which sugars 13g; Fat 8g, of which saturates 2g; Cholesterol 35mg; Calcium 44mg; Fibre 0.5g; Sodium 1.5g

# Catfish cooked in a traditional clay pot

Wonderfully easy and tasty, this southern-style dish, called *ca kho to*, is a classic in most Vietnamese homes. In the south, clay pots are regularly used for cooking and they enhance both the look and taste of this traditional dish. However, you can use any heavy pot or pan. It is delicious served with chunks of baguette to mop up the caramelized, smoky sauce at the bottom of the pot, but you could easily serve it with steamed rice or vegetables.

1 Tip the sugar into a clay pot or heavy pan, and add 15ml/1 tbsp water to wet it. Heat the sugar until it begins to brown, then add the oil and garlic.

2 Stir the *nuoc mam* into the caramel mixture and add 120ml/4fl oz/½ cup boiling water, then toss in the catfish pieces, making sure they are well coated with the sauce. Cover the pot, reduce the heat and simmer for about 5 minutes.

3 Remove the lid, season with black pepper and gently stir in the spring onions. Simmer for a further 3–4 minutes to thicken the sauce, garnish with fresh coriander, and serve immediately straight from the pot.

**serves 4**

30ml/2 tbsp sugar

15ml/1 tbsp sesame or vegetable oil

2 garlic cloves, crushed

45ml/3 tbsp *nuoc mam*

350g/12oz catfish fillets, cut
  diagonally into 2 or 3 pieces

4 spring onions (scallions), cut into
  bitesize pieces

ground black pepper

chopped fresh coriander (cilantro),
  to garnish

### clay pots

When using a traditional clay pot, always use a low to medium heat and heat the pot slowly, otherwise there is a risk of cracking it. They are designed to be used over a flame, so if using an electric stove, use a heat diffuser.

Nutritional information per portion: Energy 126Kcal/533kJ; Protein 16g; Carbohydrate 10g, of which sugars 8g; Fat 3g, of which saturates 0g; Cholesterol 40mg; Calcium 25mg; Fibre 0.2g; Sodium 0.6g

# Sour carp with tamarind, galangal, coriander and basil

This northern-style dish, made using the local river carp, is traditionally served with noodles or rice wrappers, which are folded around the fish before dipping into a sauce. Alternatively, you could simply toss the cooked fish in the herbs and serve with rice and a salad. Any freshwater fish can be used for this recipe but, because it is stirred in a wok, you will need one with firm, thick flesh. Allow plenty of time for the fish to marinate.

serves 4

500g/1¼lb carp fillets, cut into
   3 or 4 pieces
30ml/2 tbsp sesame or vegetable oil
10ml/2 tsp ground turmeric
1 small bunch each of fresh
   coriander (cilantro) and basil,
   stalks removed
20 rice wrappers or lettuce leaves
*nuoc mam* or other dipping sauce,
   to serve

FOR THE MARINADE

30ml/2 tbsp tamarind paste
15ml/1 tbsp soy sauce
juice of 1 lime
1 green or red Thai chilli,
   finely chopped
2.5cm/1in galangal root, peeled
   and grated
a few sprigs of fresh coriander,
   leaves finely chopped

1 Prepare the marinade by mixing together all the marinade ingredients in a bowl. Toss the fish pieces in the marinade, cover with clear film (plastic wrap) and chill in the refrigerator for at least 6 hours, or overnight.

2 Lift the pieces of fish out of the marinade and lay them on a plate. Heat a wok or heavy pan, add the oil and stir in the turmeric. Working quickly, so that the turmeric doesn't burn, add the fish pieces, gently moving them around the wok for 2–3 minutes. Add any remaining marinade to the pan and cook for a further 2–3 minutes, or until the pieces of fish are cooked through.

3 To serve, put the coriander and basil leaves into a small bowl, arrange the rice wrappers or lettuce leaves on a plate, and pour the dipping sauce into a bowl. Tip the cooked fish on to a serving dish and serve immediately with the herbs, rice papers and dipping sauce. To eat, tear off a bitesize piece of fish, place it on a wrapper with a few herb leaves, fold it up into a little roll, then dip it into the sauce.

Nutritional information per portion: Energy 298Kcal/1246kJ; Protein 24g; Carbohydrate 19g, of which sugars 5g; Fat 14g, of which saturates 2g; Cholesterol 121mg; Calcium 120mg; Fibre 0g; Sodium 0.3g

# Jungle fish cooked with fresh turmeric in banana leaves

Steaming fish in banana leaves over hot charcoal is a very traditional jungle method for cooking freshwater fish. Banana leaves are large and tough, and serve as basic cooking vessels and wrappers for all sorts of fish and meat. Here, the fish is cooked in six layers of leaves, allowing for the outer ones to burn. For this simple yet extremely tasty dish you could use trout, any of the catfish or carp family, or even talapia, which has been introduced to the waters of Laos and Vietnam.

**serves 4**

350g/12oz freshwater fish fillets, such as trout, cut into bitesize chunks
6 banana leaves
vegetable oil, for brushing
sticky rice, noodles or salad, to serve

FOR THE MARINADE
2 shallots
5cm/2in turmeric root, peeled and grated
2 spring onions (scallions), finely sliced
2 garlic cloves, crushed
1–2 green Thai chillies, seeded and finely chopped
15ml/1 tbsp *nuoc mam*
2.5ml/½ tsp raw cane sugar
salt and ground black pepper

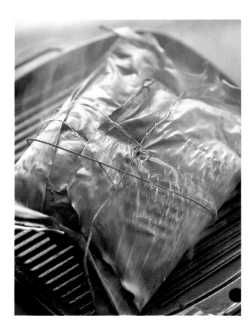

1 To make the marinade, grate the shallots into a bowl, then combine with the other marinade ingredients, seasoning with salt and pepper. Toss the chunks of fish in the marinade, making sure they are well coated, then cover and chill for 6 hours, or overnight.

2 Prepare a barbecue. Place one of the banana leaves on a flat surface and brush it with oil. Tip the marinated fish on to the banana leaf, spreading it out evenly, then fold over the sides to form an envelope. Place this envelope, fold side down, on top of another leaf and fold that one in the same manner. Repeat with the remaining leaves until they are all used up. Secure the last layer of banana leaves with a piece of bendy wire.

3 Place the banana leaf packet on the barbecue. Cook for about 20 minutes, turning it over from time to time to make sure it is cooked on both sides – the outer leaves will burn. Carefully untie the wire (it will be hot) and unravel the banana leaf packet, then serve the fish with sticky rice, noodles or salad.

## banana leaves

Banana leaves are available in some African and Asian stores and markets. If you can't find them, wrap the fish in vine leaves that have been steeped in cold water, or large flexible cabbage leaves. You can also use foil.

Nutritional information per portion: Energy 155Kcal/648kJ; Protein 18g; Carbohydrate 4g, of which sugars 2g; Fat 8g, of which saturates 1g; Cholesterol 59mg; Calcium 36mg; Fibre 0.7g; Sodium 0.2g

# Eel braised in caramel sauce with butternut squash

Although this dish is found in different parts of Vietnam, it is traditionally a northern dish and it is there, in the highlands, that it is best sampled. The eels are caught in the Red, Black and Song Ma rivers, which contribute to the local name of this dish, "three rivers eel". If you can't find eel, use mackerel. The fat rendered from these fish melts into the caramel sauce, making it deliciously velvety. It is usually served with noodles or steamed rice.

**serves 4**

45ml/3 tbsp raw cane sugar

30ml/2 tbsp soy sauce

45ml/3 tbsp *nuoc mam*

2 garlic cloves, crushed

2 dried chillies

2–3 star anise

4–5 peppercorns

350g/12oz eel on the bone, cut into
   2.5cm/1in-thick chunks

200g/7oz butternut squash, cut into
   bitesize chunks

4 spring onions (scallions), cut into
   bitesize pieces

30ml/2 tbsp sesame or vegetable oil

5cm/2in fresh root ginger, peeled
   and cut into matchsticks

salt

chopped fresh coriander (cilantro),
   to garnish

1 Put the sugar in a heavy pan or wok with 30ml/2 tbsp water, and gently heat it until it turns golden. Remove the pan from the heat and stir in the soy sauce and *nuoc mam* with 120ml/ 4fl oz/½ cup water. Add the garlic, chillies, star anise and peppercorns and return to the heat.

2 Add the eel chunks, squash and spring onions, making sure the fish is well coated in the sauce, and season with salt. Reduce the heat, cover the pan and simmer for about 20 minutes to let the eel braise gently in the sauce and steam.

3 Meanwhile, heat a small wok, tip in the oil and stir-fry the ginger until crisp and golden. Remove and drain on kitchen paper. When the eel is nicely tender, arrange it on a serving dish, scatter the crispy ginger over it, and garnish with a little fresh coriander.

Nutritional information per portion: Energy 204Kcal/857kJ; Protein 11g; Carbohydrate 20g, of which sugars 14g; Fat 10g, of which saturates 1g; Cholesterol 0mg; Calcium 76mg; Fibre 1g; Sodium 1.1g

# Grilled squid and tomatoes in a tamarind dressing

This is a lovely dish – sweet, charred squid served in a tangy dressing made with tamarind, lime and *nuoc mam*. It is best made with baby squid because they are tender and sweet. Traditionally, the squid are steamed for this dish, but their flavour is enhanced if they are cooked on a griddle, as here, or lightly charred over a barbecue. Serve while the squid is still warm.

1 Put the dressing ingredients in a bowl and stir until thoroughly mixed. Set aside.

2 Heat a ridged griddle, wipe the pan with a little oil, and griddle the tomatoes until lightly charred. Transfer them to a board, chop roughly into bitesize chunks, and place in a bowl.

3 Clean the griddle, then heat it up again and wipe with a little more oil. Griddle the squid for 2–3 minutes each side, pressing them down with a spatula, until nicely browned. Transfer to the bowl with the tomatoes, add the herbs and the dressing and toss well.

### preparing squid

To prepare squid yourself, get a firm hold of the head and pull it from the body. Reach down inside the body sac and pull out the transparent back bone, as well as any stringy parts. Rinse the body sac inside and out and pat dry. Cut the tentacles off above the eyes and add to the pile of squid you're going to cook. Discard everything else.

**serves 4**

2 large tomatoes, skinned, halved
  and seeded

500g/1¼lb fresh baby squid

1 bunch each of fresh basil,
  coriander (cilantro) and mint,
  stalks removed, leaves chopped

FOR THE DRESSING

15ml/1 tbsp tamarind paste

juice of half a lime

30ml/2 tbsp *nuoc mam*

15ml/1 tbsp raw cane sugar

1 garlic clove, crushed

2 shallots, halved and finely sliced

1–2 Serrano chillies, seeded
  and finely sliced

Nutritional information per portion: Energy 165Kcal/701kJ; Protein 22g; Carbohydrate 15g, of which sugars 10g; Fat 3g, of which saturates 1g; Cholesterol 281mg; Calcium 105mg; Fibre 1g; Sodium 0.5g

# Saigon shellfish curry

There are many variations of this delicious coconut milk-based curry all over the south of Vietnam. This recipe is made with prawns, squid and scallops but you could use any combination of shellfish, or even add chunks of filleted fish. Because there are so many Indian spice mixes and pastes sold in the southern markets, most recipes call for "curry powder". Choose a good curry powder or use garam masala. Serve with steamed rice or baguettes broken into chunks, with a few extra chillies to munch on the side.

**serves 4**

4cm/1½in fresh root ginger, peeled
  and roughly chopped

2–3 garlic cloves, roughly chopped

45ml/3 tbsp groundnut (peanut) oil

1 onion, finely sliced

2 lemon grass stalks, finely sliced

2 green or red Thai chillies, seeded
  and finely sliced

15ml/1 tbsp raw cane sugar

10ml/2 tsp Vietnamese or Thai
  shrimp paste

15ml/1 tbsp *nuoc mam*

30ml/2 tbsp curry powder
  or garam masala

550ml/18fl oz can coconut milk

juice and rind of 1 lime

4 medium-sized squid, cleaned and
  cut diagonally into 3 or 4 pieces

12 king or queen scallops, shelled

20 good-sized raw prawns (shrimp),
  shelled and deveined

1 small bunch of fresh basil,
  stalks removed

1 small bunch of fresh coriander
  (cilantro), stalks removed, leaves
  finely chopped, to garnish

salt

1 Using a mortar and pestle, grind the ginger with the garlic until it almost resembles a paste. Heat the oil in a traditional clay pot, wok or heavy pan and stir in the onion. Cook until it begins to turn brown, then stir in the garlic and ginger paste.

2 Once the aromas begin to lift from the pot, add the lemon grass, chillies and sugar. Cook briefly before adding the shrimp paste, *nuoc mam* and curry powder or garam masala. Stir well and allow the flavours to mingle and fuse over the heat for 1–2 minutes.

3 Add the coconut milk, lime juice and rind. Mix well and bring the liquid to the boil. Cook for 2–3 minutes. Season to taste with salt.

4 Gently stir in the squid, scallops and prawns and bring the liquid to the boil once more. Reduce the heat and cook gently until the shellfish turns opaque. Add the basil leaves and sprinkle the coriander over the top. Serve immediately from the pot.

**deveining prawns**

First peel off the shells, then make a shallow cut down the centre of the curved back of each prawn. Carefully pull out the black vein with a cocktail stick (toothpick) or your fingers, then rinse the deveined prawn thoroughly.

Nutritional information per portion: Energy 528Kcal/2225kJ; Protein 68g; Carbohydrate 24g, of which sugars 14g; Fat 18g, of which saturates 4g; Cholesterol 699mg; Calcium 250mg; Fibre 2.5g; Sodium 1.3g

# Mussels steamed with chilli, ginger leaves and lemon grass

This dish, called *so hap xa*, is Vietnam's version of the French classic, *moules marinière*. Here the mussels are steamed open in a herb-infused stock with lemon grass and chilli instead of wine and parsley. I enjoy both versions and was delighted to eat this one with a southern friend who dipped chunks of baguette into the cooking liquid, just like the French. This is also a popular Vietnamese method of steaming clams and snails. Beer is sometimes used instead of stock and it makes a rich, fragrant sauce.

**serves 4**

600ml/1 pint/2½ cups chicken stock
 or beer, or a mixture of the two
1 green or red Thai chilli, seeded
 and finely chopped
2 shallots, finely chopped
2–3 lemon grass stalks,
 finely chopped
1 bunch of ginger leaves
1 kg/2¼lb fresh mussels, cleaned
 and bearded
salt and ground black pepper

**ginger leaves**

Aromatic ginger leaves are hard to find outside Asia. If you can't find them, basil or coriander (cilantro) will work well in this recipe.

1 Pour the stock into a deep pan. Add the chilli, shallots, lemon grass and ginger leaves and bring it to the boil. Cover and simmer for 10–15 minutes to let the flavours infuse, then season to taste with salt and pepper.

2 Discard any mussels that remain open when sharply tapped, then tip the remaining mussels into the stock. Give the pan a good shake, cover and cook for 2 minutes, or until the mussels have opened. Discard any that remain closed. Ladle the mussels into individual bowls, making sure everyone gets some of the cooking liquid.

Nutritional information per portion: Energy 73Kcal/311kJ; Protein 11g; Carbohydrate 3g, of which sugars 1g; Fat 2g, of which saturates 0g; Cholesterol 36mg; Calcium 37mg; Fibre 0.7g; Sodium 0.7g

# Prawn and cauliflower curry with fenugreek, coconut and lime

This is a basic fisherman's curry from the southern coast of Vietnam. Simple and quick to make, it would usually be eaten from a communal bowl, or from the wok itself, and served with noodles, rice or chunks of baguette to mop up the deliciously fragrant, creamy sauce. Other popular combinations include prawns with butternut squash, pumpkin, or winter melon.

### serves 4

450g/1lb raw tiger prawns (shrimp), shelled and cleaned

juice of 1 lime

15–30ml/1–2 tbsp sesame or groundnut (peanut) oil

1 red onion, roughly chopped

2 garlic cloves, roughly chopped

2 green or red Thai chillies, seeded and roughly chopped

1 cauliflower, broken into bitesize florets

5ml/1 tsp sugar

2 star anise, pan-roasted and ground

10ml/2 tsp fenugreek, pan-roasted and ground

450ml/³/₄ pint/scant 2 cups coconut milk

1 bunch of fresh coriander (cilantro), stalks removed, leaves chopped, to garnish

salt and ground black pepper

1 In a bowl, toss the prawns in the lime juice and set aside. Heat a wok or heavy pan and add the oil. Stir in the onion, garlic and chillies. As they begin to brown, add the cauliflower, moving it around the wok for 2–3 minutes.

2 Toss in the sugar and spices. Add the coconut milk, stirring to make sure it is thoroughly combined. Reduce the heat and simmer for 10–15 minutes, or until the liquid has reduced and thickened a little. Gently add the prawns and lime juice and cook for 1–2 minutes, or until the prawns turn opaque. Season to taste, and sprinkle with fresh coriander. Serve immediately.

Nutritional information per portion: Energy 232Kcal/971kJ; Protein 25g; Carbohydrate 13g, of which sugars 12g; Fat 10g, of which saturates 2g; Cholesterol 219mg; Calcium 167mg; Fibre 2.2g; Sodium 0.5g

# Grilled prawn salad with peanuts and pomelo

This refreshing and fragrant salad is typical of the salads of central and southern Vietnam, where fruit, vegetables, meat, fish and shellfish are all tossed together in one dish. It makes a great addition to a barbecue: simply thread the prawns on to skewers to cook them or, alternatively, cook the prawns as they are on a griddle.

## serves 4

16–20 raw tiger prawns (shrimp), peeled and deveined

1 small cucumber, peeled and cut into matchsticks

1 pomelo, separated into segments and cut into bitesize pieces

1 carrot, peeled and cut into matchsticks

1 green Serrano chilli, seeded and finely sliced

30ml/2 tbsp roasted peanuts, roughly chopped

juice of half a lime

roughly 60ml/4 tbsp *nuoc cham*

vegetable oil, for griddling

1 small bunch of fresh basil, stalks removed, leaves torn

1 small bunch of coriander (cilantro), stalks removed, leaves chopped

### FOR THE MARINADE

30ml/2 tbsp *nuoc mam*

30ml/2 tbsp soy sauce

15ml/1 tbsp groundnut (peanut) oil

1 shallot, finely chopped

1 garlic clove, crushed

10ml/2 tsp raw cane sugar

1 In a wide bowl, combine all the marinade ingredients. Add the prawns, making sure they are coated, and set aside for 30 minutes.

2 Sprinkle the cucumber matchsticks with salt and leave for 15 minutes. Rinse and drain the cucumber and mix in a large bowl with the pomelo, carrot, chilli and peanuts. Add the lime juice and *nuoc cham* and toss well.

3 To barbecue, thread the marinated prawns on to wooden skewers that have been soaked in water for 30 minutes. Cook on a prepared barbecue for 2–3 minutes, turning them over from time to time. To griddle, wipe a hot griddle with a little oil, and cook the prawns on both sides until they turn opaque.

4 Once cooked, toss the prawns into the salad with the herbs and serve.

## pomelos

Larger and sweeter than grapefruits, yellow pomelos are piled high on stalls in the coastal regions, where people often peel them on a hot day to make an impromptu salad with a little salt and a few herbs. They are available in many Asian markets and stores but, if you can't find them, use a sweet, pink grapefruit instead. The zesty, refreshing flavour of the fruit makes this a lovely summer salad.

Nutritional information per portion: Energy 219Kcal/912kJ; Protein 14g; Carbohydrate 14g, of which sugars 9g; Fat 12g, of which saturates 2g; Cholesterol 98mg; Calcium 121mg; Fibre 1.4g; Sodium 0.5g

# Baked stuffed crab shells

In spite of the obvious French influence of stuffing shells and baking them, the Vietnamese have artfully made this dish their own with a combination of bean thread noodles and cloud ear mushrooms. It is time-consuming to cook the crabs yourself, so use freshly cooked crab meat from your fishmonger or supermarket. You will also need four small, empty crab shells. If you haven't eaten crab recently and kept the shells, you could ask your local fishmonger or look for some in the Asian markets. Alternatively, use individual ovenproof dishes. Bean thread noodles and cloud ear mushrooms are available in Chinese and Asian markets.

serves 4

25g/1oz dried bean thread
   (cellophane) noodles
6 dried cloud ear (wood ear)
   mushrooms
450g/1lb fresh crab meat
15ml/1 tbsp vegetable oil
10ml/2 tsp *nuoc mam*
2 shallots, finely chopped
2 garlic cloves, finely chopped
2.5cm/1in fresh root ginger,
   peeled and grated
1 small bunch of coriander (cilantro),
   stalks removed, leaves chopped
1 egg, beaten
25g/1oz/2 tbsp butter
salt and ground black pepper
finely chopped fresh dill fronds,
   to garnish
*nuoc cham*, to serve

1 Preheat the oven to 180°C/350°F/Gas 4. Soak the bean thread noodles and cloud ear mushrooms separately in bowls of lukewarm water for 15 minutes. Squeeze them dry and chop them finely.

2 In a bowl, mix together the noodles and mushrooms with the crab meat. Add the oil, *nuoc mam*, shallots, garlic, ginger and coriander. Season, then stir in the egg.

3 Spoon the mixture into four small crab shells or individual ovenproof dishes, packing it in tightly, and dot the top of each one with a little butter. Place the shells on a baking tray and cook for about 20 minutes, or until the tops are nicely browned. Garnish with dill and serve with a little *nuoc cham* to drizzle over the top.

Nutritional information per portion: Energy 289Kcal/1206kJ; Protein 26g; Carbohydrate 8g, of which sugars 2g; Fat 17g, of which saturates 5g; Cholesterol 145mg; Calcium 39mg; Fibre 24g; Sodium 0.8g

# Lobster and crab steamed in beer, with ginger and basil

In spite of its appearance on menus in restaurants that specialize in the complex and refined imperial dishes of Hue, this is one of the easiest recipes in this book. Depending on the size and availability of the lobsters and crabs, you can make it for as many people as you like, because the quantities are simple to adjust.

**serves 4**

4 uncooked lobsters, about
  450g/1lb each
4–8 uncooked crabs, about
  225g/8oz each
about 600ml/1 pint/2½ cups beer
4 spring onions (scallions), trimmed
  and chopped into long pieces
4cm/1½in fresh root ginger, peeled
  and finely sliced
2 green or red Thai chillies, seeded
  and finely sliced
3 lemon grass stalks, finely sliced
1 bunch of fresh dill, fronds chopped
1 bunch each of fresh basil and
  coriander (cilantro), stalks
  removed, leaves chopped
about 30ml/2 tbsp *nuoc mam*,
  plus extra for serving
juice of 1 lemon
salt and ground black pepper

### steaming crabs and lobsters

Whether you cook the lobsters and crabs at the same time depends on the number of people you are cooking for and the size of your steamer. However, they don't take long to cook so it is easy to steam them in batches. In the markets and restaurants of Vietnam, you can find crabs that are 60cm/24in in diameter, which may feed several people but require a huge steamer.

1 Clean the lobsters and crabs well and rub them with salt and pepper. Place half of them in a large steamer and pour the beer into the base. Scatter half the spring onions, ginger, chillies, lemon grass and herbs over the lobsters and crabs, and steam for about 10 minutes, or until the lobsters turn red. Lift them on to a serving dish. Cook the remaining half in the same way.

2 Add the lemon grass, herbs and nuoc mam to the simmering beer, stir in the lemon juice, then pour into a dipping bowl. Serve the shellfish hot, dipping the lobster and crab meat into the beer broth and adding extra splashes of *nuoc mam*, if you like.

Nutritional information per portion: Energy 264Kcal/1112kJ; Protein 48g; Carbohydrate 4g, of which sugars 1g; Fat 7g, of which saturates 1g; Cholesterol 210mg; Calcium 185mg; Fibre 0.5g; Sodium 1.3g

Meat and poultry

# Pork, beef and other meats

While the Vietnamese could happily survive on rice and fish, invariably seasoned with their treasured *nuoc mam*, they do enjoy a degree of animal protein. Most commonly, they eat pork, beef, chicken, duck, squab and quail, all of which lend themselves to marinating and grilling over charcoal for the smoky flavour it imparts and to melt the fat. Traditionally, the fat rendered from pork was important, as it was the only available cooking fat. It is still used in rural areas, where it is obtained for its desired flavour in specific dishes; otherwise vegetable, groundnut (peanut) and sesame oils have taken over the role.

Of all meats, pork is the one enjoyed most in Vietnam. The reason for this lies both in its culinary versatility and in its economic value. Every family, particularly in the countryside, can own a pig. A pig is easy and cheap to raise because it lives on scraps, it's big enough to feed a family, and every part of it is edible. The pigs from Hue are held in high esteem. Following traditional methods, they are fed rice and the fruit, leaves and bark of banana trees, which produces tender, sweet meat. A whole suckling pig, spit-roasted over an open wood fire, is a speciality reserved for wedding banquets and celebratory feasts. Each region has its own combination of herbs and spices, such as ginger, cinnamon and basil, which is rubbed into the pig. However, it is the traditional slow-roasting method that produces a candy-like, crispy skin encasing the juiciest, sweetest meat that melts in the mouth.

Beef is much enjoyed in Vietnam, but the price does vary. In the northern region, where there is good pasture, beef is reasonably priced, hence Hanoi's *bo bay mon*, a feast of seven different beef dishes. The feast is rooted in the indigenous cattle-based agriculture as well as influenced by the Mongol invaders, who loved beef. The "beef seven ways" feast begins with *bo nhung dam* (beef fondue), followed by *bo la lot* (pepper leaves stuffed with beef), *goi bo* (seared beef salad), *bo nuong xa* (grilled beef marinated in lemon grass), *cha dum* (steamed beef pâté), *cha bo* (beef patties) and finally *chao bo* (beef rice porridge), which is designed to settle the stomach. In the south, beef is expensive so it is more often reserved for special occasions. The exception to this is, of course, *pho*, the national beef noodle soup, which is served everywhere in Vietnam.

Chickens and ducks are bred throughout Vietnam, even in the densely populated neighbourhoods of Hanoi and Saigon. Bicycles with baskets full of cackling chickens and ducks wind their way through the traffic to the markets, where the birds are sold live and killed only when selected. The dead birds are then plunged into boiling water to make the feathers easier to pull off so the cook can rush home to prepare the food. Grilling on a spit or oven-roasting are the most popular methods of cooking poultry and game birds. Quails and squab are also bred for the pot in Vietnam. Quails are spit-roasted everywhere you go. Street vendors grill them to such crispy perfection that you can tuck in to the tender meat and munch the whole bird, bones and all, in a matter of minutes. Squab, on the other hand, is expensive and tends to appear as a treat at banquets or in restaurants.

Of course, nothing is wasted in the Vietnamese kitchen, so the hearts and gizzards of poultry and game birds end up in tasty stir-fries with vegetables. Delicate quail eggs are soft-boiled and braised in soy sauce; duck tongues are stir-fried with peanut saté; ducks' feet and chickens' feet are braised in coconut juice; and cooked duck eggs, containing underdeveloped embryos, are considered a delicacy as well as a source of strength.

*Beef, although relatively expensive, is one of the most popuar meats in Vietnam (right). Bamboo, lined with banana leaf, and caramelized pork (opposite); and fresh ginger, lemon grass stalks, and spring onions lightly pounded in a mortar and pestle (top).*

# Chicken and sweet potato curry with coconut and caramel sauce

This typical South-east Asian curry is simple to make and delicious to eat. Saigon is home to many stalls specializing in chicken or seafood curries. The one thing common to all is the use of a general Indian curry powder and coconut milk. Serve this curry with baguettes for mopping up the sauce, or steamed fragrant rice or noodles.

**serves 4**

45ml/3 tbsp Indian curry powder
  or garam masala
15ml/1 tbsp ground turmeric
500g/1¼lb skinless chicken thighs
  or chicken portions
25ml/1½ tbsp raw cane sugar
30ml/2 tbsp sesame oil
2 shallots, chopped
2 garlic cloves, chopped
4cm/1½ in galangal, peeled
  and chopped
2 lemon grass stalks, chopped
10ml/2 tsp chilli paste or dried
  chilli flakes
1–2 medium-sized sweet potatoes,
  peeled and cubed
45ml/3 tbsp *nuoc mam*
600ml/1 pint can coconut milk
1 small bunch each of fresh basil
  and coriander (cilantro),
  stalks removed
salt and ground black pepper

1 In a small bowl, mix together the curry powder or garam masala and the turmeric. Put the chicken thighs in a bowl and coat with half of the spice. Set aside.

2 To make the caramel sauce, heat the sugar in a small pan with 7.5ml/1½ tsp water, until the sugar dissolves and the syrup turns golden. Remove from the heat and set aside.

3 Heat a wok or wide heavy pan and add the oil. Stir-fry the shallots, garlic, galangal and lemon grass until they begin to smell fragrant. Stir in the rest of the turmeric and curry powder with the chilli paste or chilli flakes, followed by the chicken, moving it around the wok for 2–3 minutes.

4 Add the sweet potatoes, then the *nuoc mam*, caramel sauce, coconut milk and 150ml/¼ pint/ ⅔ cup water, stirring well to combine the flavours. Bring the liquid to the boil, reduce the heat

and cook for about 15 minutes or until the chicken is tender. Season with salt and pepper and stir half the basil and coriander through the curry. Garnish with the remaining herbs.

### making pork or prawn curry

You don't have to use chicken for this curry. It is equally good made with pork or prawns (shrimp), or a combination of the two. Galangal is available in Asian stores, but you can use fresh root ginger if you prefer.

# Stir-fried chicken with chillies and lemon grass

This is good, home cooking – simple food that you can enjoy as an everyday meal. There are variations of this dish, using pork or seafood, throughout South-east Asia so, for a smooth introduction to the cooking of the region, this is a good place to start. The essential elements of this dish are the fragrant lemon grass and the fire of the chillies, so add as much as you like. Serve with a table salad, rice wrappers and a dipping sauce.

serves 4

15ml/1 tbsp sugar

30ml/2 tbsp sesame or groundnut (peanut) oil

2 garlic cloves, finely chopped

2–3 green or red Thai chillies, seeded and finely chopped

2 lemon grass stalks, finely sliced

1 onion, finely sliced

350g/12oz skinless chicken breast fillets, cut into bitesize strips

30ml/2 tbsp soy sauce

15ml/1 tbsp *nuoc mam*

1 bunch of fresh coriander (cilantro), stalks removed, leaves chopped

salt and ground black pepper

*nuoc cham*, to serve

1 To make a caramel sauce, put the sugar into a small pan with a few splashes of water, but not enough to soak it. Heat it gently until the sugar has dissolved and turned golden. Set aside.

2 Heat a wok or heavy pan and add the oil. Stir in the garlic, chillies and lemon grass, and cook until they become fragrant. Add the onion and stir-fry for 1 minute, then add the chicken.

3 When the chicken begins to brown a little, add the soy sauce, *nuoc mam* and caramel sauce. Keep the chicken moving around the wok for a minute or two, then season with a little salt and pepper. Toss the fresh coriander into the chicken and serve immediately with *nuoc cham* to drizzle over it.

Nutritional information per portion: Energy 202Kcal/847kJ; Protein 22g; Carbohydrate 9g, of which sugars 7g; Fat 9g, of which saturates 1g; Cholesterol 61mg; Calcium 32mg; Fibre 0.6g; Sodium 0.8g

# Garlic-roasted quails with honey

This is a great Indo-Chinese favourite made with quails or poussins. Crispy, tender and juicy, they are simple to prepare and delicious to eat. Roast them in the oven or over a barbecue. They can be roasted whole, or split down the backbone and flattened like butterfly wings. For the New Year, *Tet*, whole chickens are marinated in similar garlicky flavourings and cooked over charcoal or in the oven. Serve with fragrant steamed rice.

**serves 4**

150ml/¼ pint/⅔ cup mushroom
 soy sauce

45ml/3 tbsp honey

15ml/1 tbsp sugar

8 garlic cloves, crushed

15ml/1 tbsp black peppercorns,
 crushed

30ml/2 tbsp sesame oil

8 quails or poussins

*nuoc cham*, to serve

**using chicken**

If you can't find quails or poussins for this dish, you could easily improvise by making it with whole chicken legs instead. The results will be just as good, and the cooking times similar.

1 In a bowl, beat the mushroom soy sauce with the honey and sugar until the sugar has dissolved. Stir in the garlic, crushed peppercorns and sesame oil. Put the quails or poussins into a dish and rub the marinade over them with your fingers. Cover and chill for at least 4 hours.

2 Preheat the oven to 230°C/450°F/Gas 8. Place the quails breast side down in a roasting pan or on a wire rack set over a baking tray, then put them in the oven for 10 minutes.

3 Take them out and turn them over so they are breast side up, baste well with the juices and return them to the oven for a further 15–20 minutes. Serve immediately with *nuoc cham* for dipping or drizzling over the meat.

Nutritional information per portion: Energy 649Kcal/2701kJ; Protein 51g; Carbohydrate 17g, of which sugars 3g; Fat 43g, of which saturates 11g; Cholesterol 250mg; Calcium 61mg; Fibre 0.2g; Sodium 0.2g

# Duck with pineapple and coriander

This is quite a fancy dish and more time-consuming than some to prepare, so it might be one reserved for celebrations. I first came across it in a restaurant, listed as duck *à l'ananas*. Clearly French-inspired, it must be the Vietnamese version of duck *à l'orange*, taking advantage of the pineapples that grow in abundance. Serve with steamed rice and a crunchy salad. Remember to allow time for the duck to marinate.

**serves 4–6**

1 small duck, skinned, trimmed
    and jointed
1 pineapple, skinned, cored and cut
    in half crossways
45ml/3 tbsp sesame or vegetable oil
4cm/1½in fresh root ginger, peeled
    and finely sliced
1 onion, sliced
salt and ground black pepper
1 bunch of fresh coriander (cilantro),
    stalks removed, to garnish

FOR THE MARINADE
3 shallots
45ml/3 tbsp soy sauce
30ml/2 tbsp *nuoc mam*
10ml/2 tsp five-spice powder
15ml/1 tbsp sugar
3 garlic cloves, crushed
1 bunch of fresh basil, stalks
    removed, leaves finely chopped

1 To make the marinade, grate the shallots into a bowl, then add the remaining marinade ingredients and beat together until the sugar has dissolved. Place the duck in a wide dish and rub with the marinade. Cover and chill for 6 hours or overnight.

2 Take one of the pineapple halves and cut into 4–6 slices, and then again into half-moons, and set aside. Take the other pineapple half and chop it to a pulp. Using your hands, squeeze all the juice from the pulp into a bowl. Discard the pulp and reserve the juice.

3 Heat 30ml/2 tbsp of the oil in a wide, heavy pot or pan. Stir in the ginger and the onion. When they begin to soften, add the duck to the pan and brown on both sides. Tip in the pineapple juice and any remaining marinade, then pour in water so that the duck is just covered. Bring the liquid to the boil, reduce the heat and simmer for about 25 minutes.

4 Meanwhile, heat the remaining oil in a heavy pan and sear the pineapple slices on both sides – you may have to do this in two batches. Add the seared pineapple to the duck, season to taste with salt and black pepper and cook for a further 5 minutes, or until the duck is tender. Arrange on a warmed serving dish, garnish with the coriander leaves and serve.

Nutritional information per portion: Energy 356Kcal/1489kJ; Protein 28g; Carbohydrate 19g, of which sugars 13g; Fat 20g, of which saturates 4g; Cholesterol 131mg; Calcium 122mg; Fibre 2g; Sodium 1.5g

# Vietnamese roast duck

This dish, *vit quay*, is Vietnam's answer to Peking duck, although here the succulent, crispy bird is enjoyed in one course, whereas the Chinese speciality is served in three courses – the crispy skin, stir-fried meat, and a broth made from the carcass. Both the Chinese and Vietnamese covet the crispy skin, which makes the dish distinctive. In a Vietnamese home, the duck is served with pickled vegetables or a salad, several dipping sauces, and either a fragrant steamed rice or a stir-fried rice made using the duck offal.

### serves 4–6

1 duck, about 2.25kg/5lb in weight

90g/3½oz fresh root ginger, peeled, roughly chopped and lightly crushed

4 garlic cloves, peeled and crushed

1 lemon grass stalk, halved and bruised

4 spring onions (scallions), halved and crushed

ginger dipping sauce, *nuoc mam gung*, pickled vegetables and salad leaves, to serve

FOR THE MARINADE

80ml/3fl oz *nuoc mam*

30ml/2 tbsp soy sauce

30ml/2 tbsp honey

15ml/1 tbsp five-spice powder

5ml/1 tsp ground ginger

1 In a bowl, beat the marinade ingredients together until the honey has dissolved. Using your fingers, rub the skin of the duck lightly to loosen it, until you can get your fingers between the skin and the meat. Rub the marinade all over the duck, inside its skin and out, then place the duck on a rack over a tray and put it in the refrigerator for 24 hours. If any of the marinade drips into the tray, rub it back over the duck.

2 Preheat the oven to 220°C/425°F/Gas 7. Stuff the ginger, garlic, lemon grass and spring onions into the duck's cavity and tie the legs with string. Using a bamboo or metal skewer, poke holes in the skin, including the legs.

3 Place the duck, breast side down, on a rack over a roasting pan and cook it in the oven for 45 minutes, basting from time to time with the juices that have dripped into the pan. After 45 minutes, turn the duck over so that it is breast side up. Baste it generously and return it to the oven for a further 45 minutes, basting it every 15 minutes. The duck is ready once the juices run clear when the bird is pierced with a skewer.

4 Serve immediately, pulling at the skin and meat with your fingers, rather than neatly carving it. Serve with ginger dipping sauce, *nuoc mam gung*, pickled vegetables and salad leaves for wrapping up the morsels.

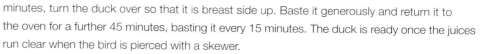

### crisping the skin

It is essential to allow the duck to rest in the refrigerator for a day and a night to let the skin dry out so that it will become crispy when cooked.

Nutritional information per portion: Energy 228Kcal/960kJ; Protein 27g; Carbohydrate 13g, of which sugars 7g; Fat 8g, of which saturates 3g; Cholesterol 131mg; Calcium 69mg; Fibre 0.3g; Sodium 1.4g

# Stir-fried pork with peanuts, lime and basil

Pork or chicken stir-fried with nuts and herbs, with a splash of citrus flavour or fish sauce, is everyday home cooking in Vietnam. The combination of lime, basil and mint in this recipe makes it particularly refreshing and tasty. Serve with steamed or sticky rice, or with rice wrappers, salad and a dipping sauce.

**serves 4**

45ml/3 tbsp vegetable or groundnut (peanut) oil

450g/1lb pork tenderloin, cut into fine strips

4 spring onions (scallions), chopped

4 garlic cloves, finely chopped

4cm/1½in fresh root ginger, finely chopped

2 green or red Thai chillies, seeded and finely chopped

100g/3½oz/generous ½ cup shelled, unsalted peanuts

grated rind and juice of 2 limes

30ml/2 tbsp *nuoc mam*

30ml/2 tbsp grated fresh coconut

25g/1oz/½ cup chopped fresh mint leaves

25g/1oz/½ cup chopped fresh basil leaves

25g/1oz/½ cup chopped fresh coriander (cilantro) leaves

1 Heat a wok or heavy pan and pour in 30ml/2 tbsp of the oil. Add the pork and sear over a high heat, until browned. Tip the meat and juices on to a plate and set aside.

2 Wipe the wok or pan clean and return to the heat. Pour in the remaining oil and add the spring onions, garlic, ginger and chillies. When the aromas begin to rise from the pan, add the peanuts and stir-fry for 1–2 minutes.

3 Tip the meat and its juices back into the wok, then stir in the lime rind and juice, followed by the *nuoc mam*. Add the fresh coconut and herbs, and serve immediately.

Nutritional information per portion: Energy 401Kcal/1668kJ; Protein 32g; Carbohydrate 7g, of which sugars 3g; Fat 27g, of which saturates 5g; Cholesterol 71mg; Calcium 42mg; Fibre 1.8g; Sodium 0.4g

# Vietnamese stir-fried pork ribs

This recipe is adapted from the classic Chinese sweet-and-sour spare ribs. The Vietnamese version, however, is a little different, with the addition of fresh basil leaves and the ubiquitous fish sauce, *nuoc mam*. This is messy finger food, requiring finger bowls, and is perfect served with sticky rice and a salad.

1 In a bowl, mix together the hoisin sauce, *nuoc mam* and five-spice powder with 15ml/1 tbsp of the oil, then set aside.

2 Bring a large pan of water to the boil, then add the pork ribs and blanch for 10 minutes. Drain them thoroughly, then set aside.

3 Heat the remaining oil in a wok. Add the crushed garlic and grated ginger and cook, stirring, until fragrant, then add the blanched pork ribs.

4 Cook for about 5 minutes, or until the ribs are nicely browned, then tip in the hoisin sauce mixture, turning the ribs so that each one is well coated. Continue stir-frying for 10–15 minutes, or until there is almost no liquid in the wok and the ribs are caramelized. Quickly add the basil and serve the ribs straight from the pan, offering dinner guests finger bowls and plenty of napkins to wipe sticky fingers.

**serves 4–6**

45ml/3 tbsp hoisin sauce

45ml/3 tbsp *nuoc mam*

10ml/2 tsp five-spice powder

45ml/3 tbsp vegetable or sesame oil

900g/2lb pork ribs

3 garlic cloves, crushed

4cm/1½in fresh root ginger, peeled and grated

1 bunch of fresh basil, stalks removed, leaves shredded

Nutritional information per portion: Energy 470Kcal/1965kJ; Protein 44g; Carbohydrate 6g, of which sugars 3g; Fat 31g, of which saturates 12g; Cholesterol 149mg; Calcium 98mg; Fibre 0.1g; Sodium 0.8g

# Grilled pork meatballs with sweet-and-sour peanut sauce

A speciality of central Vietnam, these meatballs, *nem nuong*, are best threaded on to skewers and grilled on a barbecue, but they can also be cooked under a grill. Cooked at home, or in street stalls, they are usually served with noodles and a dipping sauce. You can serve them with the sauce of your choice, although in Vietnam a peanut dipping sauce is traditional. They are also good served with chopped coriander and lime wedges.

**serves 4**

10ml/2 tsp groundnut (peanut)
  or sesame oil
4 shallots, finely chopped
2 garlic cloves, finely chopped
450g/1lb/2 cups minced
  (ground) pork
30ml/2 tbsp *nuoc mam*
10ml/2 tsp five-spice powder
10ml/2 tsp sugar
115g/4oz/2 cups breadcrumbs
  or 30ml/2 tbsp potato starch
1 bunch of fresh coriander (cilantro),
  stalks removed
salt and ground black pepper

FOR THE SAUCE

10ml/2 tsp groundnut (peanut) oil
1 garlic clove, finely chopped
1 red Thai chilli, seeded and
  finely chopped
30ml/2 tbsp roasted peanuts,
  finely chopped
15ml/1 tbsp *nuoc mam*
30ml/2 tbsp rice wine vinegar
30ml/2 tbsp hoisin sauce
60ml/4 tbsp coconut milk
100ml/3½fl oz/scant ½ cup water
5–10ml/1–2 tsp sugar

1 To make the sauce, heat the oil in a small wok or heavy pan, and stir in the garlic and chilli. When they begin to colour, add the peanuts. Stir for a few minutes, or until the natural oil from the peanuts begins to weep. Add the remaining ingredients, except the sugar, and boil the mixture for a minute. Adjust the sweetness and seasoning to your taste by adding sugar and salt, and set aside.

2 To make the meatballs, heat the oil in a wok or small pan, and stir in the shallots and garlic. When they begin to brown, remove from the heat and leave to cool. Put the minced pork into a bowl, tip in the stir-fried shallots and garlic, and add the *nuoc mam*, five-spice powder and sugar. Season with a little salt and plenty of pepper. Using your hand, knead the mixture until well combined. Cover the bowl and chill in the refrigerator for 2–3 hours.

3 Soak eight wooden skewers in water for 30 minutes. Meanwhile, knead the mixture again, then add the breadcrumbs or potato starch. Knead well to bind. Divide the mixture into 20 pieces and roll into balls. Thread the balls onto the skewers. Cook either over the barbecue or under the grill (broiler), turning the skewers from time to time.

4 Arrange the meatballs on a serving dish with coriander leaves to wrap around them, or chop the coriander and use as a garnish. Quickly reheat the sauce, stirring constantly. Transfer it to a serving bowl and serve hot with the meatballs.

### starch or breadcrumbs?

Breadcrumbs make the paste easier to work with and don't interfere with the meaty texture of the cooked ball. However, many Vietnamese prefer potato starch because it gives the meatball a smooth, springy texture, although this does make the paste very sticky to handle.

Nutritional information per portion: Energy 291Kcal/1216kJ; Protein 28g; Carbohydrate 15g, of which sugars 8g; Fat 14g, of which saturates 3g; Cholesterol 71mg; Calcium 69mg; Fibre 1.3g; Sodium 0.7g.

# Caramelized pork in bamboo

This is another Hue-inspired dish. In the preparation of so many dishes for such a demanding emperor, creativity was of the essence. Bamboo is traditionally used as a cooking vessel in central and northern Vietnam in the same way that banana leaves are in the south. In the north, eel is given this treatment because it slips whole into the bamboo cavity. You will need two bamboo tubes, about 25cm/10in long, split in half lengthways and cleaned. You can find them in some Asian stores, or try a DIY store.

### serves 4–6

1 kg/2¼lb lean pork shoulder, cut into thin strips

2 large banana leaves, torn into wide strips (or 8 sturdy leaves, such as cabbage or vine leaves)

chopped fresh coriander (cilantro), to garnish

noodles or rice and *nuoc cham*, to serve

FOR THE MARINADE

45ml/3 tbsp unrefined or muscovado (molasses) sugar

60ml/4 tbsp *nuoc mam*

3 shallots, finely chopped

6 spring onions (scallions), trimmed and finely chopped

1cm/½in piece of fresh root ginger, peeled and finely chopped

1 green or red Thai chilli, seeded and finely chopped

1 To make the marinade, gently heat the sugar in a heavy pan with 15ml/1 tbsp water, stirring constantly until it begins to caramelize. Remove from the heat and stir in the *nuoc mam*, shallots, spring onions, ginger and chilli.

2 Place the pork strips in a wide bowl or dish and tip the marinade over. Using your fingers, toss the meat in the marinade to make sure it is well coated. Cover and chill for 1–2 hours.

3 Line the inside of two of the bamboo halves with wide strips of banana leaf. Spoon the marinated pork on to the leaf, folding the edges over the top. Place the remaining bamboo halves on top to form tubes again, and then tightly wrap a wide strip of banana leaf around the outside of each tube.

4 Prepare a barbecue. Tie the bamboo parcels with string and cook over the hot barbecue for about 20 minutes. Open up the parcels, garnish the pork with coriander and serve with noodles or rice and *nuoc cham*.

### cooking in the jungle

This method of using a bamboo tube is popular in the jungles of Laos and Vietnam, where whole fish are cooked in this way over a fire. The tubes can be lined with thin, flexible cabbage leaves or vine leaves. If you can't find banana leaves, wrap the tubes in foil instead.

Nutritional information per portion: Energy 349Kcal/1469kJ; Protein 44g; Carbohydrate 17g, of which sugars 14g; Fat 12g, of which saturates 4g; Cholesterol 142mg; Calcium 71mg; Fibre 1.2g; Sodium 0.7g

# Pork cooked in a clay pot with fresh coconut

In Vietnam, this homely, rustic dish is just one of the ways of cooking the meat obtained from the family pig. It is one of those dishes in which very little effort produces a comforting and flavoursome meal. If it were being prepared for a large, hungry family, it would be served with a light soup, stir-fried or steamed rice, and a vegetable dish. If you do not have a clay pot, a heavy pan works just as well.

**serves 4**

30ml/2 tbsp sugar

30ml/2 tbsp *nuoc mam*

90ml/6 tbsp liquid from a coconut

350g/12oz pork shoulder, boned
and cut into bitesize strips

90g/3½oz fresh coconut,
finely grated

5ml/1 tsp ground black pepper

salt

chopped fresh coriander (cilantro),
to garnish

1 Put the sugar in a pan with 10ml/2 tsp water. Heat it gently until it dissolves and turns to a golden caramel colour. Remove from the heat and leave to cool.

2 In a bowl, combine the caramel with the *nuoc mam* and coconut liquid. Toss the pork strips in the mixture, making sure they are thoroughly coated, then cover and leave to marinate for 1–2 hours. While still in the bowl, add the grated coconut with the pepper, and mix well.

3 Transfer the pork and the marinating juices to a clay pot or heavy pan, and pour in 100ml/ 3½fl oz/scant ½ cup water. Bring the liquid to the boil, stir the meat gently to combine the flavours, and then reduce the heat. Cover and simmer for 5 minutes. Remove the lid and simmer for a further 5 minutes, or until the sauce has thickened a little. Season to taste with salt, and garnish with the coriander.

### extracting coconut liquid

To extract the liquid from a coconut, pierce the soft spot at the top of the fruit with a skewer and pour out the juice. You can then crack the shell and skin the flesh before grating it.

Nutritional information per portion: Energy 234Kcal/980kJ; Protein 19g; Carbohydrate 11g, of which sugars 10g; Fat 13g, of which saturates 9g; Cholesterol 56mg; Calcium 18mg; Fibre 1.8g; Sodium 0.6g

# Beef stew with star anise and basil

The Vietnamese prize this dish for breakfast, and on chilly mornings people queue up for a steaming bowl of *thit bo kho* on their way to work. In southern Vietnam, it is often served with chunks of baguette, but in the other regions it is served with noodles. For the midday or evening meal, it is served with steamed or sticky rice. Traditionally, it has an orange hue from the oil in which annatto seeds have been fried, but here the colour comes from turmeric.

1 Toss the beef in the ground turmeric and set aside. Heat a wok or heavy pan and add the oil. Stir in the shallots, garlic, chillies and lemon grass, and cook until they become fragrant.

2 Add the curry powder and all but 10ml/2 tsp of the roasted star anise, followed by the beef. Brown the beef a little, then pour in the stock or water, the *nuoc mam*, soy sauce and sugar. Stir well and bring the liquid to the boil. Reduce the heat and cook gently for about 40 minutes, or until the meat is tender and the liquid has reduced.

3 Season to taste with salt and pepper, stir in the reserved roasted star anise, and add the basil. Transfer the stew to a serving dish and garnish with the sliced onion and coriander leaves.

**serves 4–6**

500g/1¼lb lean beef, cut into
  bitesize cubes

10–15ml/2–3 tsp ground turmeric

30ml/2 tbsp sesame or vegetable oil

3 shallots, chopped

3 garlic cloves, chopped

2 red chillies, seeded and chopped

2 lemon grass stalks, cut into several
  pieces and bruised

15ml/1 tbsp curry powder

4 star anise, roasted and ground
  to a powder

700ml/scant 1¼ pints hot beef or
  chicken stock, or boiling water

45ml/3 tbsp *nuoc mam*

30ml/2 tbsp soy sauce

15ml/1 tbsp raw cane sugar

1 bunch of fresh basil, stalks removed

salt and ground black pepper

1 onion, halved and finely sliced, and
  chopped fresh coriander (cilantro)
  or leaves, to garnish

Nutritional information per portion: Energy 314Kcal/1312kJ; Protein 33g; Carbohydrate 17g, of which sugars 11g; Fat 14g, of which saturates 4g; Cholesterol 64mg; Calcium 64mg; Fibre 1.7g; Sodium 1.5g

# Vietnamese beef fondue with pineapple and anchovy dipping sauce

Introduced by the early Mongolian tribesmen, and adopted by the Chinese, *bo nhung dam* is one of the most ancient ways of cooking meat. Traditionally, it was made in a Chinese *lau*, a large turban-shaped pan containing the broth, with a charcoal stove in the centre to keep the liquid simmering. The modern method simply requires a pot over a fuel burner, just like a fondue. The Vietnamese serve this with a simple table salad, rice wrappers and a dipping sauce. Once all the meat has been cooked, the fragrant broth is poured into bowls to drink.

**serves 4–6**

30ml/2 tbsp sesame oil
1 garlic clove, crushed
2 shallots, finely chopped
2.5cm/1in fresh root ginger, peeled and finely sliced
1 lemon grass stalk, cut into several pieces and bruised
30ml/2 tbsp sugar
225ml/8½fl oz/1 cup white rice vinegar
700g/1lb 10oz beef fillet, thinly sliced into rectangular strips
salt and ground black pepper

FOR THE BEEF STOCK
450g/1lb meaty beef bones
15ml/1 tbsp soy sauce
15ml/1 tbsp *nuoc mam*
1 onion, peeled and quartered
2.5cm/1in fresh root ginger, chopped
3 cloves
1 star anise
1 cinnamon stick

FOR THE DIPPING SAUCE
15ml/1 tbsp white rice vinegar
juice of 1 lime
5ml/1 tsp sugar
1 garlic clove, peeled and chopped
2 Thai chillies, seeded and chopped
12 preserved anchovy fillets, drained
2 slices of pineapple, centre removed and flesh chopped

1 To make the stock, put the beef bones into a deep pan with the other ingredients and cover with 900ml/1½ pints/3¾ cups water. Bring the water to the boil, reduce the heat and simmer, covered, for 1–2 hours. Remove the lid, turn up the heat and gently boil the stock for a further 30–40 minutes, or until it has reduced. Strain and season with salt. Measure out 300ml/½ pint/1¼ cups and set aside.

2 Meanwhile, make the dipping sauce. In a bowl, mix the vinegar and lime juice with the sugar, until the sugar dissolves. Using a mortar and pestle, crush the garlic and chillies together to form a paste. Add the anchovy fillets and pound them to a paste, then add the pineapple and pound it to a pulp. Stir in the vinegar mixture, and set aside.

3 When ready to eat, put 15ml/1 tbsp of the sesame oil into a heavy pan, wok or fondue pot. Quickly stir-fry the garlic, shallots, ginger and lemon grass until fragrant and golden, then add the sugar, vinegar, beef stock and the remaining sesame oil. Bring the liquid to the boil, stirring constantly until the sugar has dissolved. Season to taste with salt and plenty of freshly ground black pepper.

4 Transfer the pan or fondue to a lighted burner at the table. Lay the beef fillet on a serving dish, and put the dipping sauce in a serving bowl. Using chopsticks or fondue forks, each person cooks their own meat in the broth and dips it into the sauce. After all the meat has been cooked, serve the broth.

### traditional ingredients

To make the meal truly Vietnamese, provide rice wrappers and chopped vegetables and herbs to make little bundles to dip in the sauce. Traditionally, any meat is used for this dish – pork, chicken, and even shellfish and eel.

# Beef saté

The spicy peanut paste, saté, is a great favourite in South-east Asia. Although it is more associated with Thai cooking, it is thought to have originated in India. In southern Vietnam, it is used for grilling and stir-frying meats and seafood, as well as for dressing egg noodles and spiking marinades. This is a great barbecue dish that works just as well with pork tenderloin, chicken breast, prawns or shrimp. Jars of saté are now available in many stores but they taste nothing like the homemade paste, which you can pep up with as much garlic and chilli as you like.

1 To make the saté, heat the oil in a heavy pan and stir in the garlic until it begins to colour. Add the chillies, curry powder and peanuts and stir over a gentle heat until the mixture forms a paste. Remove from the heat and leave to cool.

2 Put the beef into a bowl. Beat the groundnut oil into the saté and tip the mixture on to the beef. Mix well, so that the beef is evenly coated. Soak four to six wooden skewers in water for 30 minutes. Prepare a barbecue. Thread the meat on to the skewers and cook for 2–3 minutes on each side. Serve the meat with the herb leaves for wrapping.

### beef saté salad

The beef is also delicious served with a salad, rice wrappers and a light dipping sauce.

**serves 4–6**

500g/1¼lb beef sirloin, sliced
   against the grain in bitesize pieces

15ml/1 tbsp groundnut (peanut) oil

1 bunch each of fresh coriander
   (cilantro) and mint, stalks removed

FOR THE SATÉ

60ml/4 tbsp groundnut (peanut)
   or vegetable oil

4–5 garlic cloves, crushed

4–5 dried Serrano chillies, seeded
   and ground

5–10ml/1–2 tsp curry powder

50g/2oz/⅓ cup roasted peanuts,
   finely ground

Nutritional information per portion: Energy 433Kcal/1798kJ; Protein 34g; Carbohydrate 4g, of which sugars 1g; Fat 31g, of which saturates 7g; Cholesterol 64mg; Calcium 68mg; Fibre 1.5g; Sodium 0.1g

# Seared beef salad in a lime dressing

This dish, *goi bo*, is a great Indo-Chinese favourite and versions of it are enjoyed in Vietnam, Thailand, Cambodia and Laos. It is also one of the traditional dishes that appear in the *bo bay mon* – beef seven ways feast – in which seven different beef dishes are served. For the most delicious result, it is worth buying an excellent-quality piece of tender fillet steak because the meat is only just seared before being dressed in the spicy, fragrant lime dressing and tossed in a crunchy salad of beansprouts and fresh, aromatic herbs.

**serves 4**

about 7.5ml/1½ tsp vegetable oil
450g/1lb beef fillet, cut into steaks
  2.5cm/1in thick
115g/4oz/½ cup beansprouts
1 bunch each fresh basil and mint,
stalks removed, leaves shredded
1 lime, cut into quarters, to serve

FOR THE DRESSING
juice (about 80ml/3fl oz) and rind
  of 2 limes
30ml/2 tbsp *nuoc mam*
30ml/2 tbsp raw cane sugar
2 garlic cloves, crushed
2 lemon grass stalks, very
  finely sliced
2 green Serrano chillies, seeded
  and finely sliced

1 To make the dressing, beat the lime juice, rind and *nuoc mam* in a bowl with the sugar, until the sugar dissolves. Stir in the garlic, lemon grass and chillies and set aside.

2 Tip a little oil into a heavy pan and rub it over the base with a piece of kitchen paper. Heat the pan and sear the steaks for 1–2 minutes each side. Transfer them to a board and leave to cool a little. Using a sharp knife, cut the meat into thin, flat slices. Toss the slices in the dressing, cover and leave to marinate for 1–2 hours.

3 Drain the meat of any excess juice and transfer it to a wide serving bowl. Add the beansprouts and herbs and toss it all together. Serve with extra lime to squeeze over.

Nutritional information per portion: Energy 233Kcal/979kJ; Protein 26g; Carbohydrate 12g, of which sugars 9g; Fat 9g, of which saturates 3g; Cholesterol 69mg; Calcium 74mg; Fibre 0.5g; Sodium 0.4g

Vegetable dishes and salads

# Fresh and healthy

By and large, the Vietnamese are voracious omnivores, and although they are keen to eat anything that crawls, swims or flies, they also have a high regard for vegetables. Raw, stir-fried, braised, pickled or salted, vegetables are worked into every meal. Almost every dish includes a few vegetables but, in addition, there may be a vegetable side dish, salad, pickled vegetables or lettuce leaves to wrap around the food. A Vietnamese meal must be balanced, with vegetable, protein and starch.

In the warm southern region of Vietnam, the growing season is long and abundant, providing the regional cuisine with a vast choice of indigenous, and adopted, roots and leaves with which to make exciting salads. With such an emphasis on spice for other parts of the meal, these fresh, crunchy salads add a refreshing touch. In the cool north, vegetables are more often cooked and preserved, borrowing ancient Chinese methods.

For centuries, the port of Da Nang in the centre of Vietnam has been involved in overseas trade, including the arrival of New World fruits and vegetables such as tomatoes, chillies, potatoes, corn and pineapples. The new vegetables have acclimatized to the regional growing seasons, and have been so deliciously incorporated into the traditional cuisine that you would think they had always been there. Among the vegetables that make a regular appearance on the Vietnamese table are beansprouts, bamboo shoots, aubergines (eggplant), bitter melons, taro, water spinach, daikon (mooli), mustard greens, lotus roots, a variety of Chinese mushrooms, the turnip-like jicama, beans, cabbage and banana blossoms. The Vietnamese have also adopted vegetables and fruit from the West, such as avocados and asparagus, which probably came with the French.

Whenever possible, the Vietnamese prefer raw vegetables and herbs in a variety of salads, as in the popular Vietnamese table salad *sa lach dia*, or pickled to munch on with grilled meats, fish and shellfish. Otherwise, vegetables are generally stir-fried or braised. Of all the vegetables, water spinach could be considered the national favourite. It grows quickly and profusely in the north and the south, appearing in a dish almost daily. Stir-fried with garlic and *nuoc mam*, it makes a delicious side dish.

On the full moon (the 15th day of the lunar month) or on new moon days (the last day of the lunar month), some Vietnamese avoid eating meat altogether. On these days some restaurants and many of the food stalls prepare purely vegetarian meals, even excluding *nuoc mam*. The Buddhist monks of the Mahayana

tradition, on the other hand, adhere to a strict vegetarian diet all the time, although some components, such as tofu, are moulded or pressed to look like pieces of meat in the dish. One of the best-known Vietnamese vegetarian dishes is called "Buddha's delight", a combination of stir-fried cauliflower, mange touts (snow peas), (bell) peppers, carrots and bamboo shoots, which, although extremely colourful to look at, can be quite bland to taste. In general, for strict vegetarian cooking, ginger, garlic and other herbs and spices are required to enhance the flavours, and soy sauce can replace the fish sauce, *nuoc mam*. Bearing this in mind, almost all the recipes in this chapter could be changed into vegetarian dishes by replacing the meat with tofu and the *nuoc mam* with soy or hoisin sauce.

*Asian aubergines (eggplants) are smaller than common European varieties, some are like apples and some are as small as peas (right). Salad wrapped in lettuce leaves (opposite) and lotus stems (top).*

# Jungle curry

Variations of this fiery, flavoursome vegetarian curry can be found all over southern Vietnam. A favourite with the Buddhist monks and often sold from countryside stalls, it can be served with plain rice or noodles, or chunks of crusty bread. Jungle curry should be fiery, almost dominated by the chilli. In Vietnam it is often eaten for breakfast as a sustaining dish to set you up for the day, but it is also a great pick-me-up at any other time of day.

**serves 4**

30ml/2 tbsp vegetable oil

2 onions, roughly chopped

2 lemon grass stalks, roughly chopped and bruised

3–4 green Thai chillies, seeded and finely sliced

4cm/1½in galangal or fresh root ginger, peeled and chopped

2–3 carrots, peeled, halved lengthways and sliced

115g/4oz long green beans

grated rind of 1 lime

10ml/2 tsp soy sauce

15ml/1 tbsp rice vinegar

10ml/2 tsp *nuoc mam*

5ml/1 tsp black peppercorns, crushed with a mortar and pestle

15ml/1 tbsp sugar

5–10ml/1–2 tsp ground turmeric

115g/4oz canned bamboo shoots

75g/3oz spinach, steamed and roughly chopped

150ml/¼ pint/⅔ cup coconut milk

salt

chopped fresh coriander (cilantro) and mint leaves, to garnish

1 Heat a wok or heavy pan and add the oil. Once hot, stir in the onions, lemon grass, chillies and galangal or ginger. Add the carrots and beans with the lime rind and cook for 1–2 minutes.

2 Stir in the soy sauce, rice vinegar and *nuoc mam*. Add the crushed peppercorns, sugar and turmeric, then stir in the bamboo shoots and the spinach.

3 Pour in the coconut milk and blend the mixture together. Cook for about 10 minutes, then season with salt. Serve hot, garnished with fresh coriander and mint.

### yard long beans

Also known as snake beans or asparagus beans, these extremely long green beans can be found all over South-east Asia. They may grow up to 40cm/16in long and can be found in Asian stores. There are two common varieties – pale green and darker green – the latter have the better flavour. When buying, choose young, narrow specimens with underdeveloped seeds, as these will be the most tender. They do not have strings, and preparation is simply trimming and chopping them into short lengths. As they mature, long beans can become quite tough. Try to use yard long beans within 3 days of purchase, before they turn yellow.

Nutritional information per portion: Energy 159Kcal/660kJ; Protein 3g; Carbohydrate 19g, of which sugars 16g; Fat 8g, of which saturates 1g; Cholesterol 0mg; Calcium 68mg; Fibre 3.7g; Sodium 0.2g

# Luffa squash with mushrooms, spring onions and coriander

Winter gourds, such as pumpkins, bitter melons, luffa squash and a variety of other squash that come under the kabocha umbrella, are popular vegetables for soups and braised dishes. Any of these vegetables can be used for this side dish, but luffa squash – also known as ridged gourd – is easy to work with and is available in most Asian markets. It resembles a long courgette, usually lighter in colour and with ridges from one end to the other.

**serves 4**

about 750g/1lb 10oz luffa
   squash, peeled
30–45ml/2–3 tbsp groundnut
   (peanut) or sesame oil
2 shallots, halved and sliced
2 garlic cloves, finely chopped
115g/4oz/1½ cups button (white)
   mushrooms, quartered
15ml/1 tbsp mushroom sauce
10ml/2 tsp soy sauce
4 spring onions (scallions), chopped
   into 2cm/³⁄₄in pieces
25g/1oz/½ cup chopped fresh
   coriander (cilantro) leaves

1 Cut the luffa squash diagonally into 2cm/³⁄₄in-thick pieces. Heat the oil in a wok or heavy
   pan. Stir in the shallots and garlic and, once they begin to colour, add the mushrooms.
2 Add the mushroom and soy sauces, followed by the sliced squash. Reduce the heat and
   cover the wok or pan, allowing the squash to soften in the steam for a few minutes.
   Add the spring onions and coriander and serve immediately.

Nutritional information per portion: Energy 194Kcal/800kJ; Protein 3g; Carbohydrate 19g, of which sugars 3g; Fat 12g, of which saturates 2g; Cholesterol 0mg; Calcium 31mg; Fibre 5.1g; Sodium 0.1g

# Spicy tofu with lemon grass, basil and peanuts

This very tasty dish is a wonderful way to cook tofu. In Vietnam, you might find that aromatic pepper leaves are used as the herb element but, because these are quite difficult to find outside South-east Asia, I use basil leaves. Equally, lime, coriander or curry leaves would work well in this simple stir-fry that can be served on its own with rice or with other vegetable dishes and salads. For the best results, leave the tofu to marinate for the full hour.

**serves 3–4**

3 lemon grass stalks, finely chopped

45ml/3 tbsp soy sauce

1–2 red Serrano chillies, seeded and finely chopped

2 garlic cloves, crushed

5ml/1 tsp ground turmeric

10ml/2 tsp sugar

300g/11oz tofu, rinsed, drained, patted dry and cut into bitesize cubes

30ml/2 tbsp groundnut (peanut) oil

45ml/3 tbsp roasted peanuts, chopped

1 bunch fresh basil, stalks removed

salt

1 In a bowl, mix together the lemon grass, soy sauce, chillies, garlic, turmeric and sugar until the sugar has dissolved. Add a little salt to taste and add the tofu, making sure it is well coated. Leave to marinate for 1 hour.

2 Heat a wok or heavy pan. Pour in the oil, and stir in the marinated tofu, turning it frequently to make sure it is evenly cooked. Add the peanuts and most of the basil leaves.

3 Tip the tofu on to a serving dish, scatter the remaining basil leaves over the top and serve hot or at room temperature.

Nutritional information per portion: Energy 120Kcal/500kJ; Protein 3g; Carbohydrate 5g, of which sugars 3g; Fat 10g, of which saturates 2g; Cholesterol 0mg; Calcium 36mg; Fibre 3.3g; Sodium 0.2g

# Smoked aubergine with a spring onion and chilli dressing

One of the wonderful things about aubergines is that they can be placed in the flames of a fire, or over hot charcoal, or directly over the gas flame of a stove, and still taste great. This way of smoking or roasting them has its roots in North Africa, the Middle East, India and across South-east Asia, producing infinite variations of delicious dips, purées and salads. This Vietnamese version is served as a side salad to meat and poultry dishes.

**serves 4**

**2 aubergines (eggplants)**

**30ml/2 tbsp groundnut (peanut)
    or vegetable oil**

**2 spring onions (scallions),
    finely sliced**

**1–2 red Serrano chillies, seeded
    and finely sliced**

**15ml/1 tbsp *nuoc mam***

**25g/1oz/½ cup fresh basil leaves**

**salt**

**15ml/1 tbsp roasted peanuts,
    crushed**

***nuoc cham*, to serve**

1 Place the aubergines over a barbecue or under a hot grill (broiler), or directly on to a gas flame and, turning them from time to time, cook until soft when pressed. Carefully lift them by the stalk and put them into a plastic bag to sweat for 1 minute.

2 Holding the aubergines by the stalk once again, carefully peel off the skin under cold running water. Gently squeeze the excess water from the peeled flesh, remove the stalk and pull the flesh apart in long strips. Place these strips in a serving dish.

3 Heat the oil in a small pan and quickly stir in the spring onions. Remove the pan from the heat and stir in the chillies, *nuoc mam*, basil leaves and a little salt to taste. Pour this dressing over the aubergines, toss gently and sprinkle the peanuts over the top.

4 Serve at room temperature and, for those who like a little extra fire, splash on some *nuoc cham*.

### cooking aubergines on a barbecue

If you grill the aubergines outside over a barbecue, the flesh is even easier to remove. Simply slit the tough, blackened skins and scoop out the flesh using a spoon, then pull the flesh apart into strips and continue as before.

# Stir-fried spinach with nuoc cham

In the Vietnamese countryside this simple dish is a favourite with roadside vendors, who make it with water spinach. I have used ordinary garden spinach in this version but really any spring greens, Savoy cabbage, kale or Asian cabbages would work, although the larger, tougher leaves should be blanched first. Asparagus and cauliflower can also be stir-fried in a similar manner. Serve any of these versions as a simple side dish to meat or fish, or with other vegetable dishes of your choice.

1 Heat a wok or large pan and add the oil. Stir in the garlic and chillies and cook for 1 minute, then add the spinach leaves and toss around the pan.

2 Once the spinach leaves begin to wilt, add the *nuoc cham*, making sure it coats the spinach. Season to taste with salt and pepper and serve immediately.

**serves 3–4**

30ml/2 tbsp groundnut (peanut)
  or sesame oil

2 garlic cloves, finely chopped

1–2 green or red Thai chillies, seeded
  and finely chopped

500g/1¼lb fresh, young
  spinach leaves

45ml/3 tbsp *nuoc cham*

salt and ground black pepper

**water spinach**

Also known as swamp cabbage, water convolvulus and morning glory, water spinach is the most widely eaten vegetable in Vietnam. It has long, narrow green leaves and a delicious flavour.

Nutritional information per portion: Energy 120Kcal/500kJ; Protein 3g; Carbohydrate 5g, of which sugars 3g; Fat 10g, of which saturates 2g; Cholesterol 0mg; Calcium 36mg; Fibre 3.3g; Sodium 0.2g

# Sweet-and-sour cucumber with chillies, coriander and mint

Short, fat cucumbers are a common sight in the markets of Vietnam. Because they are so refreshing, they are either peeled and eaten as a snack or sliced and dressed with lime and herbs for a delightful accompaniment to meat, poultry and seafood dishes. This salad is a great addition to the summer barbecue or salad table.

**serves 4–6**

2 cucumbers

30ml/2 tbsp sugar

100ml/3½fl oz/scant ½ cup
   rice vinegar

juice of half a lime

1–2 green Thai chillies, seeded
   and finely sliced

2 shallots, halved and finely sliced

1 small bunch each of fresh
   coriander (cilantro) and mint,
   stalks removed, leaves finely
   chopped

salt

1 Use a vegetable peeler to remove strips of the cucumber peel. Halve the cucumber lengthways and cut into slices. Place the slices on a plate and sprinkle with a little salt. Leave to stand for 15 minutes, then rinse and drain.

2 In a bowl, mix the sugar with the vinegar until it has dissolved, then stir in the lime juice and a little salt to taste.

3 Add the chillies, shallots, herbs and cucumber to the dressing and leave to stand for 15–20 minutes to allow the flavours to mingle before serving.

Nutritional information per portion: Energy 59Kcal/248kJ; Protein 2g; Carbohydrate 12g, of which sugars 11g; Fat 0g, of which saturates 0g; Cholesterol 0mg; Calcium 63mg; Fibre 0.8g; Sodium 0.2g

# Salad rolls with pumpkin, tofu, peanuts and basil

This is one of the best Vietnamese "do-it-yourself" dishes. You place all the ingredients on the table with the rice wrappers for everyone to assemble their own rolls. Salad rolls are popular snack food in Saigon and other towns of the south, where the *bo bia* (salad roll) carts come out in the warm weather. Pumpkin, squash, courgette or aubergine could be used in the filling, and cured Chinese sausage is often included instead of tofu.

**serves 4–5**

about 30ml/2 tbsp groundnut
 (peanut) or sesame oil

175g/6oz tofu, rinsed and patted dry

4 shallots, halved and sliced

2 garlic cloves, finely chopped

350g/12oz pumpkin flesh, cut
 into strips

1 carrot, cut into strips

15ml/1 tbsp soy sauce

3–4 green Thai chillies, seeded
 and finely sliced

1 small, crispy lettuce, torn
 into strips

1 bunch fresh basil, stalks removed

115g/4oz/²⁄₃ cup roasted
 peanuts, chopped

100ml/3½fl oz/scant ½ cup
 hoisin sauce

20 dried rice wrappers

salt

*nuoc cham* (optional), to serve

1 Heat a heavy pan and smear with a little oil. Place the block of tofu in the pan and sear on both sides. Transfer to a plate and cut into thin strips.

2 Heat 30ml/2 tbsp oil in the pan and stir in the shallots and garlic. Add the pumpkin and carrot, then pour in the soy sauce and 120ml/4fl oz/½ cup water. Add a little salt to taste and cook gently until the vegetables have softened but still have a bite to them.

3 Meanwhile, arrange the tofu, chillies, lettuce, basil, roasted peanuts and hoisin sauce in separate dishes and put them on the table. Fill a bowl with hot water and place it in the middle of the table, or fill a small bowl for each person, and place the stack of rice wrappers beside it. Tip the cooked vegetable mixture into a dish and add to the bowls of ingredients on the table.

4 To eat, take a rice wrapper and dip it in the water for a few seconds to soften. Lay the wrapper flat on the table or on a plate and, just off-centre, spread a few strips of lettuce, followed by the pumpkin mixture, some tofu, a sprinkling of chillies, a drizzle of hoisin sauce, some basil leaves and peanuts, layering the ingredients in a neat stack. Pull the shorter edge of the wrapper (the side with filling on it) up over the stack, tuck in the sides and roll into a tight cylinder. Dip the roll into *nuoc cham*, if you like.

Nutritional information per portion: Energy 402Kcal/1669kJ; Protein 14g; Carbohydrate 29g, of which sugars 13g; Fat 26g, of which saturates 5g; Cholesterol 0mg; Calcium 321mg; Fibre 4.1g; Sodium 0.4g

# Green mango salad

Although the sweet orange and yellow mangoes and papayas are devoured in vast quantities when ripe and juicy, they are also popular when unripe and green. Piled high in baskets in the markets, they are sold as a vegetable rather than a fruit because the tart and crunchy texture is sought after for salads and stews. This simple salad has a refreshingly tangy, sweet flavour and a lovely texture, and is delicious served with steamed or stir-fried prawns, and with grilled or seared beef. Green mangoes have dark green skins and light green flesh and can be found in Chinese and Asian markets.

**serves 4**

450g/1lb green mangoes

rind and juice of 2 limes

30ml/2 tbsp sugar

30ml/2 tbsp *nuoc mam*

2 green Thai chillies, seeded
  and finely sliced

1 small bunch of fresh coriander
  (cilantro), stalks removed,
  finely chopped

salt

1 Peel, halve and stone (pit) the mangoes, and slice them into thin strips.
2 In a bowl, mix together the lime juice and rind, sugar and *nuoc mam*. Add the mango strips with the chillies and coriander. Add salt to taste and leave to stand for 20 minutes to allow the flavours to mingle before serving.

Nutritional information per portion: Energy 92Kcal/391kJ; Protein 1g; Carbohydrate 22g, of which sugars 15g; Fat 0g, of which saturates 0g; Cholesterol 0mg; Calcium 32mg; Fibre 33g; Sodium 0.5g

# Vietnamese table salad

The Vietnamese table salad, *sa lach dia*, can vary from a bowl of fresh, leafy herbs to a more tropical combination of beansprouts, water chestnuts, mangoes, bananas, star fruit, peanuts and rice noodles. Traditionally, a table salad is served to accompany the classic finger foods such as spring rolls (*cha gio*) and pork or shrimp balls, where pieces of the salad might be wrapped around a meaty morsel. When the salad is served on its own, the vegetables and fruit are usually folded into little packets using lettuce leaves or rice wrappers, and then dipped in a sauce, or added bit by bit to bowls of rice or noodles. The arrangement of a salad is simple and attractive.

**serves 4–6**

1 crunchy lettuce, with
 leaves separated
half a cucumber, peeled
 and thinly sliced
1–2 carrots, peeled and finely sliced
200g/7oz/scant 1 cup beansprouts
1–2 unripe star fruit, finely sliced
 into stars
1–2 green bananas, finely sliced
1 firm papaya, cut in half, seeds
 removed, peeled and finely sliced
1 bunch each of fresh mint and basil,
 stalks removed
juice of 1 lime

1 Arrange the salad ingredients attractively on a plate, with the lettuce leaves on one side so that they can be used as wrappers.
2 Squeeze the lime juice over the fruits, particularly the bananas to help them retain their colour, and place the salad in the middle of the table.

Nutritional information per portion: Energy 108Kcal/455kJ; Protein 4g; Carbohydrate 21g, of which sugars 12g; Fat 1g, of which saturates 0g; Cholesterol 0mg; Calcium 110mg; Fibre 42g; Sodium 0.02g

# Lotus stem salad with shallots and shredded fresh basil

The Vietnamese love the lotus plant because it symbolizes purity and perfection. Every part of the plant is used: the flowers are laid at shrines and temples; the stamens are steeped to make a soothing tea; the seeds are dried for desserts and cakes; and the stems and roots are sliced up for soups and salads, where they absorb the flavours of the dressing while retaining a crunchy texture. You may be lucky enough to find fresh lotus stems in an Asian market, or, as here, you can use the ones preserved in brine.

**serves 4**

half a cucumber

225g/8oz jar preserved lotus stems,
   drained and cut into 5cm/2in strips

2 shallots, finely sliced

25g/1oz/½ cup fresh basil
   leaves, shredded

fresh coriander (cilantro) leaves,
   to garnish

FOR THE DRESSING

juice of 1 lime

15–30ml/1–2 tbsp *nuoc mam*

1 red Thai chilli, seeded
   and finely chopped

1 garlic clove, crushed

15ml/1 tbsp sugar

1 To make the dressing, mix together the dressing ingredients in a bowl and set aside.

2 Peel the cucumber and cut it into thin 5cm/2in strips. Soak the strips in cold salted water for 20 minutes. Put the lotus stems into a bowl of water. Using a pair of chopsticks, stir the water constantly so that the loose fibres of the stems wrap around the sticks. Drain the stems and put them in a bowl.

3 Drain the cucumber strips and add them to the bowl, then add the shallots, shredded basil leaves and the prepared dressing. Leave the salad to marinate for 20 minutes before serving. Garnish with fresh coriander leaves.

## lotus roots

If you cannot find the stems, lotus roots make a good substitute and are readily available in Asian markets. They grow in sausage-like links, each one about 18–23cm/7–9in long. Once the mud that coats them has been washed off, a pale beige-pink skin is revealed. When buying fresh lotus roots, choose ones that feel heavy for their size, as this is an indication that they are full of liquid. They should be peeled and soaked in water with a little lemon juice before being added to the salad.

Nutritional information per portion: Energy 43Kcal/181kJ; Protein 1g; Carbohydrate 9g, of which sugars 6g; Fat 0g, of which saturates 0g; Cholesterol 0mg; Calcium 40mg; Fibre 0.5g; Sodium 0.3g

Sweet snacks

# Sweet treats

The Vietnamese love sweet flavours, and sugar is used throughout the Vietnamese diet. Even the savoury dishes often include sugar or a sweet sauce to balance the sour or spicy tastes. Despite this, though, the Vietnamese rarely finish a meal with a sweet dessert. Traditionally, fruit is reserved for the end of a meal to cleanse the palate or aid the digestion – and with such a selection of exotic and tropical fruits on offer, it is no surprise. Puddings and cakes are enjoyed, but they are nibbled as snacks.

Many different types of fruit are grown in Vietnam, including milky-white lychees, large, sweet pineapples, fragrant, red arbutus and the flowery rambutan. You will also find buttery mangoes and papayas, green bananas, juicy, brown-skinned longans, dragon fruit, cinnamon apples, pretty star fruit, watermelon-sized jackfruit with bright yellow flesh, and zesty citrus fruit, such as pomelo. Coconuts are plentiful – both ripened and immature – although the soft, jelly-like flesh and fresher milk of the young ones are preferred for snacking on. Most distinctive of all is the infamous spiky, football-sized durian, which is considered the king of fruit – in spite of the fact that although it tastes like heaven, it smells like hell.

The Vietnamese word for sweet pudding is *che*. In Saigon, there are as many stalls for *che* as there are for noodles and *pho*, and they all look much the same: lots of big metal pots containing delicious-smelling mixtures attended by a noisy vendor yelling to the masses. The *che* stall might serve a moist rice pudding with taro root and coconut milk; or perhaps sweet dumplings filled with creamy mung beans in a ginger-scented broth; or for those looking to quench their thirst there's the popular sweet snack drink *che ba mau*, made with mung beans, red beans, coconut milk and crushed ice. Another sweet snack found everywhere is *banh*, which could be described as a Vietnamese cake. Generally, in the same manner as their savoury counterparts, the sweet *banh* are prepared with sticky rice or rice flour, stuffed with sweet mung bean paste or shredded coconut, steamed inside a banana leaf wrapping and served with hot tea. Examples of this type of *banh* are the pyramid-shaped *banh it nhan dau* sold on the Mekong Delta crossings and the *banh deo* which are filled with candied fruit and eaten during the mid-autumn festival.

The more sophisticated Vietnamese desserts reveal a distinctly French influence and tend to be restaurant and café specialities rather than home-cooked dishes. These include the Gallic classics such as crème caramel – made in Vietnam with coconut milk – and thin, creamy flans, flambéed fritters and tropical ice creams. One Vietnamese ice cream invention called *kem dua*, *kem trai due*, which is a mix of ice cream and candied fruit, combined with the jelly-like flesh of immature coconuts and served in the baby coconut shell, is truly delightful. From the Chinese, the Vietnamese

*Coconut crème caramel is a popular dish in Vietnam, served both as a snack and in more sophisticated restaurants (above). Star fruit, papaya and fresh lychees (opposite) and fried bananas (top).*

have adopted the idea of sweet soups, such as *che chuoi*, using bananas and coconut. The old imperial city of Hue in central Vietnam specializes in sweet soups. There are also sugary dessert-like snacks made with pulses, and cakes and puddings made with root vegetables, such as taro and sweet potato. Root vegetables and jungle fruits are also poached in a fragrant syrup; avocados are eaten as a sweet snack, puréed, sweetened with sugar and served on ice, and the local pandanus leaf is used for flavouring.

# Jungle fruits in lemon grass syrup

This exotic and refreshing fruit salad can be made with any combination of tropical fruits – just go for a good balance of colour, flavour and texture. You can also flavour the syrup with ginger rather than lemon grass, if liked.

1 To make the syrup, put 225ml/7½fl oz/1 cup water into a heavy pan with the sugar and bruised lemon grass stalks. Bring the liquid to the boil, stirring constantly until the sugar has dissolved, then reduce the heat and simmer for 10–15 minutes. Leave to cool.

2 Peel and halve the papaya, remove the seeds and slice the flesh crossways. Peel the pineapple and slice it into rounds. Remove the core and cut each round in half.

3 Put all the fruit into a bowl. Pour the syrup, including the lemon grass stalks, over the top and toss lightly to combine. Cover and chill for at least 6 hours, or overnight, to allow the flavours to mingle. Remove the lemon grass stalks before serving.

**serves 6**

1 firm papaya
1 small pineapple
2 small star fruit, sliced into
   stars
1 can preserved lychees
   or 12 fresh lychees, peeled
   and stoned (pitted)
2 firm yellow or green bananas,
   peeled and cut diagonally
   into slices

FOR THE SYRUP

115g/4oz/generous ½ cup caster
   (superfine) sugar
2 lemon grass stalks, bruised

Nutritional information per portion: Energy 160Kcal/683kJ; Protein 1g; Carbohydrate 41g, of which sugars 40g; Fat 0g, of which saturates 0g; Cholesterol 0mg; Calcium 22mg; Fibre 1.8g; Sodium 0g

# Coconut sorbet

Deliciously refreshing and cooling, this tropical sorbet can be found in different versions all over South-east Asia. Other classic Vietnamese sorbets include lychee, pineapple, watermelon and lemon grass.

**serves 6**

175g/6oz/scant 1 cup caster (superfine) sugar
120ml/4fl oz/½ cup coconut milk
50g/2oz/⅔ cup grated or desiccated (dry unsweetened shredded) coconut
a squeeze of lime juice
fresh mint leaves, to decorate

1 Place the sugar in a heavy pan and add 200ml/7fl oz/scant 1 cup water. Bring to the boil, stirring constantly, until the sugar has dissolved completely. Reduce the heat and simmer for 5 minutes to make a light syrup.

2 Stir the coconut milk into the syrup, along with most of the coconut and the lime juice. Pour the mixture into a bowl or freezer container and freeze for 1 hour.

3 Take the sorbet out of the freezer and beat it, or blend it in a food processor, until smooth and creamy, then return it to the freezer and leave until frozen.

4 Before serving, allow the sorbet to stand at room temperature for 10–15 minutes to soften slightly. Serve in small bowls and decorate with the remaining coconut and the mint leaves.

Nutritional information per portion: Energy 170Kcal/718kJ; Protein 1g; Carbohydrate 32g, of which sugars 32g; Fat 5g, of which saturates 5g; Cholesterol 4mg; Calcium 11mg; Fibre 1.1g; Sodium 0g

# Durian ice cream

Following the French influence of creamy, custard-based ice creams, the Vietnamese have come up with some exciting recipes using local fruits and flavourings. Because the notoriously pungent durian is one of their favourite fruits, it is no surprise that it is used to make ice cream too.

**serves 8**

6 egg yolks

115g/4oz/generous ½ cup caster (superfine) sugar

500ml/17fl oz/2¼ cups full-fat (whole) milk

350g/12oz durian flesh

300ml/½ pint/1¼ cups double (heavy) cream

### durian

The Vietnamese name for this strong-smelling fruit is *saw rieg* (one's sorrow), but the sweet, creamy, yellow flesh of the fruit is indisputably delicious. The problem is getting to this nectar. With its tough, brownish skin covered in thorns, and the overwhelming smell as you cut into it, you might wonder if it's worth the effort. Be assured though – it definitely is. Just hold your nose and persevere.

1 In a bowl, whisk the egg yolks and sugar together until light and frothy. In a heavy pan, heat the milk to just below boiling point, then pour it slowly into the egg mixture, whisking constantly.

2 Strain the milk and egg mixture into a heavy pan and place it over the heat, stirring constantly, until it thickens and forms a creamy custard. Leave to cool.

3 Purée the durian flesh. Strain the custard into a bowl, then whisk in the cream. Fold in the durian flesh, making sure it is thoroughly combined.

4 Pour the mixture into an ice cream maker and churn until frozen. Alternatively, pour into a freezerproof container and freeze for 4 hours, beating twice with a fork or whisking with an electric mixer to break up the ice crystals.

Nutritional information per portion: Energy 392Kcal/1692kJ; Protein 32g; Carbohydrate 69g, of which sugars 32g; Fat 27g, of which saturates 15g; Cholesterol 211mg; Calcium 117mg; Fibre 0g; Sodium 0.04g

# Star anise ice cream

Spices play an important role in the ice creams from the south of Vietnam, with their lively tastes of cinnamon, clove, star anise and pandanus leaf. This syrup-based ice cream has a clean, warming taste of star anise that will punctuate the end of a spicy Vietnamese meal perfectly, leaving you with a really exotic taste in your mouth.

1 In a heavy pan, heat the cream with the star anise to just below boiling point, then remove from the heat and leave to infuse until cool.

2 In another pan, dissolve the sugar in 150ml/¼ pint/⅔ cup water, stirring constantly. Bring the liquid to the boil for a few minutes to form a light syrup, then leave to cool for 1 minute.

3 Whisk the egg yolks in a bowl. Trickle in the hot syrup, whisking constantly, until the mixture becomes mousse-like. Pour in the infused cream through a sieve, and continue to whisk.

4 Pour the mixture into an ice cream maker and churn until frozen. Alternatively, pour the mixture into a freezerproof container and freeze for 4 hours, beating twice with a fork or whisking with an electric mixer to break up the ice crystals. To serve, dust with a little ground star anise.

**serves 6–8**

500ml/17fl oz/2¼ cups double
  (heavy) cream
8 whole star anise
90g/3½oz/½ cup caster
  (superfine) sugar
4 large (US extra large)
  egg yolks
ground star anise, to decorate

Nutritional information per portion: Energy 393Kcal/1623kJ; Protein 3g; Carbohydrate 14g, of which sugars 14g; Fat 37g, of which saturates 22g; Cholesterol 198mg; Calcium 45mg; Fibre 0g; Sodium 0.01g

# Coconut crème caramel

There is no mistaking the French influence on this dessert. Based on the classic French dessert, crème caramel, this Vietnamese version is made with coconut milk. Hugely popular throughout Vietnam, it is served both as a snack and as a more sophisticated dessert in restaurants, where it is sometimes garnished with mint leaves or toasted coconut. You can use this recipe to make one large dessert or six small ones.

**serves 4–6**

4 large (US extra large) eggs

4 egg yolks

50g/2oz/¼ cup caster
    (superfine) sugar

600ml/1 pint/2½ cups
    coconut milk

30ml/2 tbsp finely grated fresh
    coconut and a few small fresh
    mint leaves, to decorate

FOR THE CARAMEL

150g/5oz/¾ cup caster
    (superfine) sugar

1 Preheat the oven to 160°C/325°F/Gas 3. To make the caramel, heat the sugar and 75ml/5 tbsp water in a heavy pan, stirring constantly until the sugar dissolves. Bring to the boil and, without stirring, let the mixture bubble until it is dark golden and almost like treacle.

2 Tip the caramel mixture into an ovenproof dish, or six individual ramekins, tilting the dish to swirl it around so that it covers the bottom and sides – you will need to do this quickly. Put the dish aside and leave the caramel to set.

3 In a bowl, beat the eggs and egg yolks with the sugar. Heat the coconut milk, but don't allow it to boil, and gradually pour it on to the egg mixture, while constantly beating. Pour the mixture through a sieve over the caramel in the dish.

4 Set the dish or ramekins in a bain-marie – a roasting pan or wide oven dish half-filled with water. Place it in the oven for about 50 minutes, or until set with a little wobble – check with your fingertips. Leave the dish to cool then chill in the refrigerator for at least 6 hours, or overnight.

5 To serve, loosen the custard around the sides using a thin, sharp knife. Place a flat serving plate over the top and invert the custard, holding on to the dish and plate at the same time. Shake it a

little before removing the inverted dish, then lift it off as the caramel drizzles down the sides and forms a puddle around the pudding. Decorate with a little fresh coconut and small mint leaves, and serve.

**French flavours**

Crème caramel is particularly popular in the city of Hanoi, where it has been adopted with enthusiasm. Another popular French import to Vietnam is mayonnaise.

Nutritional information per portion: Energy 256Kcal/1078kJ; Protein 9g; Carbohydrate 31g, of which sugars 31g; Fat 11g, of which saturates 4g; Cholesterol 338mg; Calcium 79mg; Fibre 0.4g; Sodium 0.2g

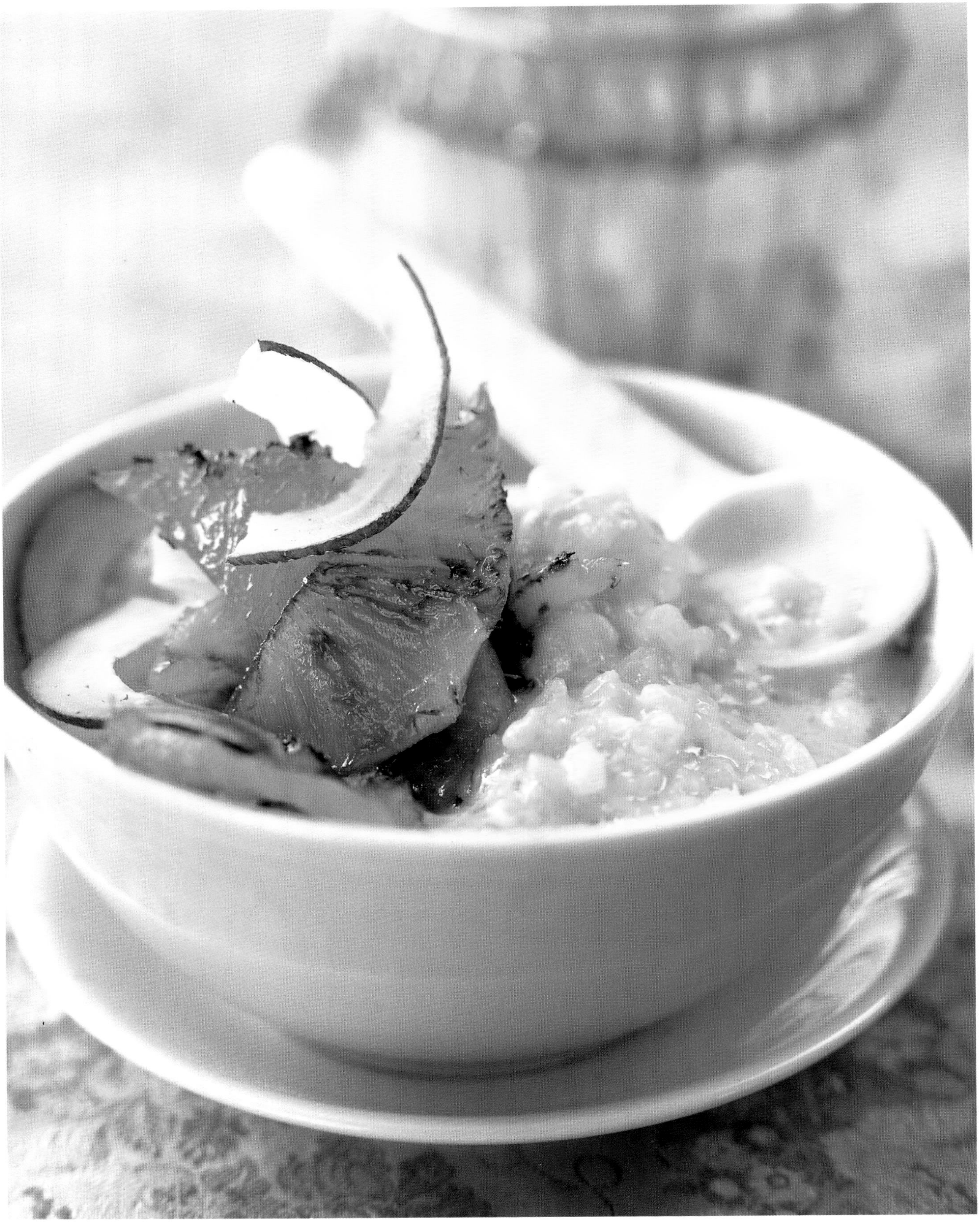

# Baked coconut rice pudding with sautéed pineapple and ginger

This rice pudding made with coconut milk and toasted coconut is another French-inspired dessert. When served in the Vietnamese home, it might be accompanied by fruits in syrup, or stir-fried bananas or pineapple. It needs long, slow cooking in a low oven, so be sure to allow plenty of time to make it. It is well worth the wait.

**serves 4–6**

90g/3½oz/½ cup pudding rice

600ml/1 pint/2½ cups coconut milk

300ml/½ pint/1¼ cups full-fat (whole) milk

75g/2¾oz/scant ½ cup caster (superfine) sugar

25g/1oz/2 tbsp butter, plus extra for greasing

45–60ml/3–4 tbsp fresh or desiccated (dry unsweetened shredded) coconut, toasted

1 small, sweet pineapple

30ml/2 tbsp sesame oil

5cm/2in piece of fresh root ginger, peeled and grated

shavings of toasted coconut, to garnish

1 Preheat the oven to 150°C/300°F/Gas 2. Grease an ovenproof dish. In a bowl, mix the rice with the coconut milk, milk and 50g/2oz/¼ cup sugar and tip it into the ovenproof dish. Dot pieces of butter over the top and place the dish in the oven.

2 After 30 minutes, take the dish out and gently stir in the toasted coconut. Return it to the oven for a further 1½ hours, or until almost all the milk is absorbed and a golden skin has formed on top of the pudding.

3 Using a sharp knife, peel the pineapple and remove the core, then cut the flesh into bitesize cubes. Towards the end of the cooking time, heat the oil in a wok or heavy pan. Stir in the ginger and, as the aroma is released, add the pineapple cubes, turning them over to sear on both sides. Sprinkle with the remaining sugar and continue to cook until the pineapple is slightly caramelized. Serve the rice pudding spooned into bowls and topped with the hot, caramelized pineapple and shavings of toasted coconut.

## sweet treats

The Vietnamese love sticky rice and mung bean desserts and always sprinkle a little extra sugar over the top to serve. For a slightly different flavour, serve the rice pudding with slices of seared mango or banana instead of the sautéed pineapple.

Nutritional information per portion: Energy 414Kcal/1735kJ; Protein 6g; Carbohydrate 56g, of which sugars 39g; Fat 19g, of which saturates 9g; Cholesterol 24mg; Calcium 156mg; Fibre 1.6g; Sodium 0.2g

# Sweet mung bean soup

In Hue, sweet soups are a great favourite. In the restaurants and parks along the Perfume River, people pause for a while to enjoy a bowl of sweet soup made with different sorts of beans, rice, tapioca, bananas or even lotus seeds with root vegetables such as taro. This recipe is for the classic favourite made with the traditional mung beans, *che dau xanh*. On a chilly day, it has the same warming and comforting effect as a bowl of porridge.

**serves 4–6**
225g/8oz/1 cup skinned split mung
   beans, soaked in water for 3 hours
   and drained
500ml/17fl oz/2¼ cups
   coconut milk
about 50g/2oz/¼ cup caster
   (superfine) sugar
toasted coconut shavings (optional),
   to serve

### mung beans
Be sure to buy the bright yellow, peeled, split mung beans for this soup rather than the whole green ones. If you do buy the whole green ones, they will need to be peeled before cooking, which is a dull and time-consuming task.

1 Put the mung beans in a pan and pour in 500ml/17fl oz/2¼ cups water. Bring the water to the
   boil, stirring constantly, then reduce the heat and simmer until all the water has been absorbed.
   Press the beans through a sieve, or purée them in a blender.
2 In a heavy pan, heat the coconut milk with the sugar, stirring until the sugar has dissolved. Gently
   stir in the puréed mung beans, making sure the soup is thoroughly mixed and heated through.
   Serve hot in warmed bowls sprinkled with toasted coconut shavings, if liked.

Nutritional information per portion: Energy 240Kcal/1025kJ; Protein 15g; Carbohydrate 45g, of which sugars 20g; Fat 1g, of which saturates 0g; Cholesterol 0mg; Calcium 57mg; Fibre 0g; Sodium 0.1g

# Cassava sweet

This type of sweet and sticky snack is usually served with a cup of light jasmine tea. More like an Indian *helva* than a cake, this recipe can also be made using sweet potatoes or yams in place of the cassava.

1 Preheat the oven to 190°C/375°F/Gas 5 and grease a baking dish with some butter. In a bowl, whisk the coconut milk with the sugar, aniseed and salt, until the sugar has dissolved.

2 Beat the grated cassava root into the coconut mixture and pour into the greased baking dish. Place it in the oven and bake for about 1 hour, or until nicely golden on top. Leave the sweet to cool in the dish before serving.

## preparing cassava

To prepare the cassava for grating, use a sharp knife to slit the whole length of the root and then carefully peel off the skin. Simply grate the peeled root using a coarse grater.

**serves 6–8**

butter, for greasing
350ml/12fl oz/1½ cups coconut milk
115g/4oz/generous ½ cup
  palm sugar
2.5ml/½ tsp ground aniseed
pinch of salt
675g/1½lb cassava root, peeled
  and grated

Nutritional information per portion: Energy 254Kcal/1086kJ; Protein 1g; Carbohydrate 64g, of which sugars 25g; Fat 1g, of which saturates 1g; Cholesterol 2mg; Calcium 39mg; Fibre 1.8g; Sodium 0.2g

# Deep-fried dumplings filled with sweetened mung beans

Adopted from a Chinese recipe, sweet and savoury rice dumplings are popular snacks in Vietnam. In this dish, *dau xanh vung*, the potato and rice-flour dumplings are stuffed with the classic Vietnamese filling of sweetened mung bean paste and then rolled in sesame seeds. When cooked at home, they are often served with fragrant jasmine tea.

### serves 6

100g/3½oz/scant ½ cup split mung
  beans, soaked for 6 hours
  and drained

115g/4oz/generous ½ cup caster
  (superfine) sugar

300g/10½oz/scant 3 cups glutinous
  rice flour

50g/2oz/½ cup rice flour

1 medium potato, boiled in its skin,
  peeled and mashed

about 75g/3oz/6 tbsp
  sesame seeds

vegetable oil, for deep-frying

1 Put the mung beans in a pan with half the sugar and pour in 450ml/¾ pint/scant 2 cups of water. Bring the water to the boil, stirring constantly until the sugar has dissolved. Reduce the heat and simmer until the mung beans are soft – you may need to add more water if the beans are becoming dry, otherwise they will burn on the bottom of the pan. Once they are soft and all the water has been absorbed, pound the beans to a smooth paste and leave to cool.

2 In a bowl, beat the flours and remaining sugar into the mashed potato. Add about 200ml/7fl oz/scant 1 cup water to bind the mixture into a moist dough. Divide the dough into 24 pieces, roll each one into a small ball, then flatten with the heel of your hand to make a disc and lay out on a lightly floured board.

3 Divide the mung bean paste into 24 small balls and place a ball in the centre of each dough disc. Fold over the edges of the dough and shape into a ball. Tip the sesame seeds on to a plate and roll each filled dough ball in them until evenly coated.

4 Heat enough oil in a wok or heavy pan for deep-frying. Fry the balls in batches by dropping them gently into the oil and rolling them around with chopsticks or tongs to make sure they are crisp and golden all over. Drain on kitchen paper and serve warm.

### stuffing and steaming

These little fried dumplings may also be filled with a sweetened red bean paste, sweetened taro root or, as in China, a lotus paste. Alternatively, the dumplings can be steamed and then soaked in syrup. Both versions are very popular throughout Vietnam.

Nutritional information per portion: Energy 321Kcal/1346kJ; Protein 7g; Carbohydrate 40g, of which sugars 21g; Fat 16g, of which saturates 2g; Cholesterol 0mg; Calcium 104mg; Fibre 3.1g; Sodium 0g

# Vietnamese fried bananas

Wherever you go in Vietnam, you will find fried bananas. They are eaten hot, straight from the pan, as a quick and tasty sweet snack. More elaborately, they might be combined with one of the lovely French-style ice creams, such as creamy, pandanus-flavoured *kem*, which is rather like vanilla ice cream, or toasted coconut *kem*. The Vietnamese are fortunate enough to have a number of different types of banana to choose from, and the local beer makes the tastiest batter for coating the fruit.

**serves 4**

4 ripe but firm sweet bananas
vegetable oil, for deep-frying
caster (superfine) sugar
   for sprinkling

FOR THE BATTER
115g/4oz/1 cup rice or plain
   (all-purpose) flour
2.5ml/½ tsp baking powder
45ml/3 tbsp caster (superfine) sugar
150ml/¼ pint/⅔ cup water
150ml/¼ pint/⅔ cup beer

1 To make the batter, sift the flour with the baking powder into a bowl. Add the sugar and beat in a little of the water and beer to make a smooth paste. Gradually beat in the rest of the water and beer to form a thick batter. Leave to stand for 20 minutes.

2 Peel the bananas and cut them in half crossways and in half again, lengthways. Pour enough oil for deep-frying into a wok or a heavy, shallow pan.

3 Cook the bananas in batches, so they don't stick together in the pan. Dip each one into the batter, making sure it is well coated, and slip it into the hot oil. Use tongs or chopsticks for turning and make sure each piece is nicely crisp and golden all over.

4 Drain the fried bananas on kitchen paper and sprinkle them with sugar. Serve immediately.

### sweet soups

The Vietnamese also use bananas to make a sweet soup that is served hot or at room temperature. Made with tapioca, coconut milk and chunks of ripe banana, these soups are very nourishing and may be enjoyed at any time of day.

Nutritional information per portion: Energy 290Kcal/1211kJ; Protein 3g; Carbohydrate 48g, of which sugars 22g; Fat 9g, of which saturates 1g; Cholesterol 0mg; Calcium 22mg; Fibre 1.7g; Sodium 0.6g

# Index

AUTHOR'S ACKNOWLEDGEMENTS

First, I would like to thank the gorgeous Peter Grant at Frank's,
Singapore, who first set my mind on this part of the world. His
knowledge, stories and encouragement have been invaluable.
I would also like to thank his friends, Douglas Toidy and Le
Huong, at their Vung Tau fish farm. They were marvellous hosts
and guides, whetting my appetite to learn more and more.
For additional research, the Rough Guide was a constant
companion, and I thoroughly enjoyed A Vietnamese Feast by
AK and Authentic Vietnamese Cooking by Corinne Trang.

With a tight deadline cast into a busy life, I feel compelled
to thank a few people closer to home: Paul Bennington of
Tomintoul Computers, who patiently sorted out my computer
hiccups at any time of day and night; my good buddies,
Angus and Ainsley, who always make a happy, welcoming
home for my children; and little Yasmin and Zeki, who had to
put up with a grumpy mum.

For the best spices and pastes from South-east Asia and
other parts of the world, please look up:
www.seasonedpioneers.com, or contact :
Seasoned Pioneers Ltd, 101 Summers Road, Brunswick
Business Park, Liverpool L3 4BJ – Tel: +44 (0)151 709 9330.
They can deliver to any location in the world.

PUBLISHER'S ACKNOWLEDGEMENTS

All photography is by Martin Brigdale, apart from the following
images: pages 6 and 9 – Robert Harding Picture Library; page
7 and page 8 – Powerstock.